RESULTS-DRIVEN MANAGEMENT
Implementing
PERFORMANCE-BASED MEASURES
in Community Corrections

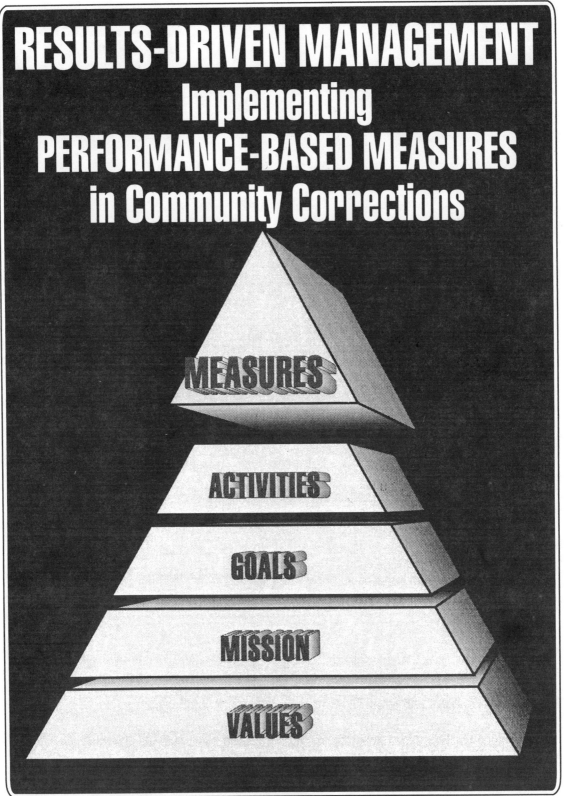

The American Probation and Parole Association

Order additional copies of this monograph by calling (606)244-8207.

The research conducted for this monograph was supported under award #93-IJ-CX-004 from the National Institute of Justice, Office of Justice Programs, U.S. Department of Justice.

This manual was prepared in cooperation with the Council of State Governments who provides project staff and secretariat services to the American Probation and Parole Association.

Points of view in this document are those of the author(s) and do not necessarily represent the official position of the U.S. Department of Justice.

AUTHORS

Harry N. Boone Jr., Ph.D.

Betsy Fulton

with

Ann H. Crowe
and
Gregory Markley

American Probation and Parole Association

APPA'S VISION

We see a fair, just and safe society where community partnerships are restoring hope by embracing a balance of prevention, intervention and advocacy.

ACKNOWLEDGEMENTS

An advisory board consisting of prominent academicians and corrections practitioners provided invaluable consultation in the development and writing of this Monograph. They were Don Andrews, Professor, Department of Psychology, Carleton University, Ottawa, Canada; Todd Clear, Professor, School of Criminal Justice, Rutgers University, Newark, New Jersey; Ronald Corbett, Deputy Commissioner, Massachusetts Office of the Commissioner of Probation; Dorothy Faust, Deputy Chief of Programs, Maricopa County, Arizona Adult Probation Department; Vernon Fogg, Administrator of Probation Programs, Colorado State Judicial Department; Alan Harland, Associate Professor, Criminal Justice Department, Temple University, Philadelphia, Pennsylvania; Joan Petersilia, Professor, School of Social Ecology, University of California, Irvine; Paula Pumphrey, Director, Arkansas Department of Community Punishment; and Alan Schuman, President, American Probation and Parole Association.

Advisory board members Alan Harland, Dorothy Faust, and Joan Petersilia along with William Burrell, Chief of Supervision Services for the New Jersey Administrative Office of the Courts and Carl Wicklund, former Court Services Director for the Dodge-Fillmore-Olmsted Community Corrections System in Rochester, Minnesota reviewed the initial draft of the Monograph and offered recommendations for improvements.

Voncile Gowdy served as the NIJ project monitor, providing support and assistance throughout the project.

TABLE OF CONTENTS

LIST OF FIGURES/TABLES

RESULTS-DRIVEN MANAGEMENT:

IMPLEMENTING PERFORMANCE-BASED MEASURES IN COMMUNITY CORRECTIONS

INTRODUCTION

The 1990s have been a period of growth for community corrections, not just in terms of increasing offender populations and the concomitant responsibilities, but in terms of integrity and professionalism. Over the past decade, a sound knowledge base has been established upon which to build credible programs and improve operations. As community corrections faces increasing challenges, it becomes even more imperative that the exploration for efficient and effective practices continues. This monograph, offers a strategy for continuing that exploration -- a model for the development and implementation of performance-based measures for community corrections.

What are performance-based measures? In the simplest of terms, performance-based measures provide agencies with a mechanism for assessing what agencies do and how well they do it. There are two types of performance-based measures: 1) process measures (i.e., was the program implemented as designed); and 2) outcome measures (i.e., did the program or practices achieve the desired results). As discussed in Module I, Chapter Two, both types of measures are required to accurately assess a program's effectiveness. Performance-based measurements move agencies away from merely counting activities (e.g., the number of referrals to services) to measuring results (e.g., did the services address offender needs).

Why are performance-based measures important? The continuing prevalence of poverty, illiteracy, substance abuse, and violence along with escalating government spending is causing taxpayers to question what they are getting for

their money. This scrutiny creates pressure for legislators who control government purse strings to address these human service areas in cost-effective ways. As the complexity of the budgetary process increases for legislators, it will increase for all government agencies. Instead of waiting for the budgetary axe to fall, community corrections agencies must arm themselves with information that demonstrates their worth in order to compete for limited financial resources.

The definition of "worth" however is changing. To date, community corrections has been fairly successful in securing limited funds based on the number of offenders on probation or parole, the number of offenders with a drug or alcohol problem, or the number of activities performed within probation and parole. A safety net has been created by focusing on inputs rather than outputs. But this safety net is quickly disintegrating; the focus is now on "fixing" the problem, not on how many times something is done to how many people. The public is demanding governmental accountability in the form of quantifiable, performance-based measures -- they want results.

Community corrections cannot be expected to "fix" the crime problem, no more than institutional corrections or any other component of the criminal justice system. That must be made clear to the voting public. But community corrections can, and does, play a crucial role in public safety. That must also be made clear. By failing to demonstrate results, community corrections agencies do themselves a great disservice. These agencies provide many services that reduce the likelihood of offenders under their supervision committing future crimes. They provide treatment and services, conduct surveillance and enforce court/parole board orders. The connection between these services and public safety is often lost because of a failure to measure and communicate results. By measuring the *outcomes* of these activities, agencies can better assess the effectiveness of various supervision strategies and program components and begin to understand what it is that leads to a reduction in recidivism -- the *ultimate* goal of any correctional program. These and other rationale for performance-based measurement strategies are discussed more fully in Module I, Chapter One.

How will the model assist agencies in developing a performance-based measurement strategy? As described in Module I, Chapter Two, performance-based measurement can be complex. The proposed model is designed to assist community corrections agencies and professionals in exploring the following three fundamental questions leading to the development of performance-based measures:

1) *What are the agency's values, mission and goals?* The clarification of an agency's values, mission and goals are essential first steps in developing performance-based measurements. An examination of these program elements should guide agency personnel toward the identification of both process and outcome measures that assess and communicate what community corrections agencies do.

2) *What specific activities does the agency perform in the name of goal achievement and how effectively are these activities performed?* Agencies should examine the basic theory, or philosophy, upon which probation/parole activities are based to determine if they are aligned with stated goals. Process measures, such as the number and type of contacts or

the style of interaction between officers and offenders, are needed to determine if activities and services are being delivered according to specifications.

3) *Are these activities leading to goal achievement?* Once it has been determined that programs and practices are being implemented as designed, the impact of these programs and practices can be assessed. For example, are control-oriented activities such as electronic monitoring or house arrest serving as a deterrent to criminal activity; and are the drug treatment programs being used by an agency leading to reduced drug abuse and offender change? The ultimate question may then be, how do these program components relate to recidivism?

Module II provides a hypothetical community corrections agency to demonstrate the model's utility. Chapters Three to Eight, within this module, address goal-specific applications of the model. The proposed model is not designed to dictate appropriate goals and outcome measures. Instead it is designed to provide a structured format for agencies to use in exploring important organizational issues and examining methods for monitoring, evaluating and communicating agency performance and accomplishments. Each agency must work through the process on its own, with the involvement of key stakeholders, to arrive at a performance-based measurement strategy that accurately reflects the agency's organizational values and mission.

How can a performance-based measurement strategy improve agency practices? Performance-based measures offer community corrections agencies and professionals a chance to define their true values and translate them into action and results. They indicate what an agency is doing to support their organizational mission and goals and how effectively they are doing it. They provide a basis for program modification and improvements and a mechanism for linking employee evaluation to the agency's mission. As discussed in Module III, by implementing a system of performance-based measures, community corrections agencies position themselves as learning organizations and demonstrate commitment to achieving their stated goals.

Agency administrators, unit supervisors and line officers will benefit from careful examination of this monograph. Measuring performance allows for organizational and professional growth; demonstrating results justifies resources and establishes credibility. A performance-based measurement strategy puts control over programs and practices in the hands of agency personnel. Given the proper learning environment and a system of structured feedback, community corrections agencies and personnel will discover ways to improve outcomes and achieve desired goals.

MODULE I

CRITICAL ISSUES IN PERFORMANCE-BASED MEASUREMENT

MODULE I

CRITICAL ISSUES IN PERFORMANCE-BASED MEASUREMENT

Module Overview

This first module encompasses two chapters designed to lay the groundwork for developing and implementing a system of performance-based measurements in community corrections. *Chapter One: Rationale for Performance-Based Measurements* explores the organizational benefits derived from measuring results in community corrections. It describes how performance-based measurements can capture the essence of what agencies do and communicate it both internally to agency personnel and externally to funding sources, decisionmakers and the public. Also discussed is the primary advantage of performance-based measurements -- the opportunity they provide for engaging staff in ongoing improvements to community corrections programs and practices. *Chapter Two: A Model for Performance-Based Measurement* encourages the exploration of critical organizational issues associated with measuring program effectiveness. It examines the complexities involved in performance-based measurement and translates these complexities into a user-friendly model for developing such a system within community corrections agencies. At the conclusion of this chapter, the reader will understand the importance of aligning key organizational practices to the achievement of desired outcomes.

CHAPTER ONE

RATIONALE FOR PERFORMANCE-BASED MEASURES

Introduction

The decade of the nineties is an era of change and restructuring; one in which fiscal constraints and demands for governmental accountability make a publicly funded organization's continued existence less dependent on tradition and more dependent on accomplishments. In order to compete for public funds, community corrections agencies must be proactive and take steps toward proving the value of their existence.

Performance-based measurements contribute knowledge about what community corrections agencies are doing and how effectively they are doing it. Specifically, they provide:

• justification for organizational existence;

• a method for measuring short-term and inter-mediate outcomes;

• a method for enhancing the value of cost-benefit analysis as a decisionmaking tool;

• an opportunity for results-oriented management;

• a mechanism for clearly communicating the role of community corrections in public safety; and

• an ongoing system of monitoring and evaluation.

These items are essential to continued improvements in agency operations. The manner in which performance-based measures can contribute to their development and to the enhancement of community corrections will be the topic of discussion throughout this chapter.

Organizational Existence

Based on probation and parole facts such as those reported in Figures 1 - 4, community corrections clearly represents a "growth industry." Growth in the availability of resources, however, has not kept pace with the number of offenders; cutbacks are taking place across the nation. The necessary supervision resources simply are not available for managing these large numbers of offenders. In a survey of probation and parole professionals conducted in 1992, diminishing or inadequate resources was identified as one of the major issues confronting community corrections professionals in the nineties (American Probation and Parole Association [APPA], 1993a, 1993b). The fiscal trend reported in Figure 5 shows why this is a concern. The level of total direct corrections expenditures for probation and parole services decreased nearly seven percent from 1977 to 1990.

In response to this fiscal trend, correctional organizations have been scrambling to find less expensive ways to manage the offender population. A wide range of intermediate sanction programs has been introduced throughout the last decade due to prison crowding, a shift in judicial philosophy toward these programs, and broad support from key criminal justice stakeholders. But just as regular supervision caseloads are beyond capacity, intermediate sanction programs will also begin to overflow, keeping

Figure 1 - Probation Population

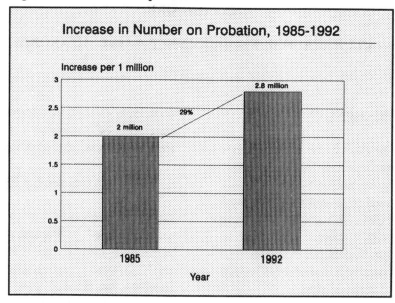

Source: Camp, G. M., & Camp, C. G. (1993). *The corrections yearbook: Probation and parole.* South Salem, New York: Criminal Justice Institute.

Figure 2 - Parole Population

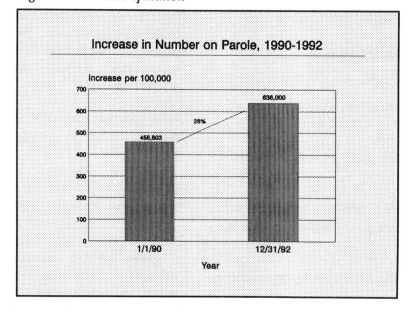

Source: Camp, G. M., & Camp, C. G. (1993). *The corrections yearbook: Probation and parole.* South Salem, New York: Criminal Justice Institute.

Figure 3 - Probation Caseloads

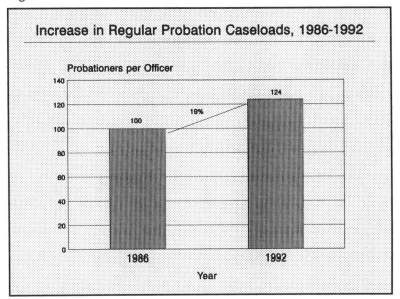

Source: Camp, G. M., & Camp, C. G. (1993). *The corrections yearbook: Probation and parole.* South Salem, New York: Criminal Justice Institute.

Figure 4 - Parole Caseloads

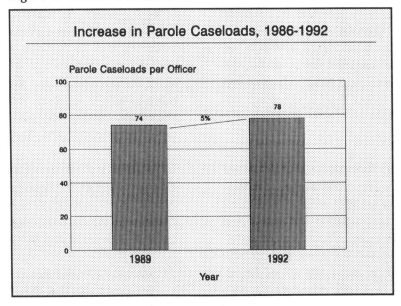

Source: Camp, G. M., & Camp, C. G. (1993). *The corrections yearbook: Probation and parole.* South Salem, New York: Criminal Justice Institute.

Figure 5 - Expenditures

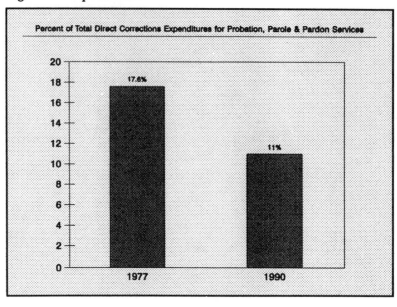

Source: Lindgren, S. (1992). *Justice expenditure and employment, 1990.* Bureau of Justice Statistics Bulletin.
Washington, DC: U.S. Department of Justice.

probation and parole in a reactive position. These trends are likely to continue unless community corrections agencies can provide strong arguments for why these large numbers of offenders cannot be managed safely within the community with the current level of human and financial resources.

Defining Boundaries

Probation and parole "boundaries," as discussed here, include caseload sizes and workload issues. The past decade has brought an increased number of individuals on probation and parole and additional responsibilities. The aggregate statistics reported in Figures 1-4 mask the extreme gravity of the situation; caseloads in Los Angeles County are up to 2,000 offenders per two officer team, and New York City has shifted thousands of offenders to the newly developed Kiosk System, an automated check-in system. Other urban areas are demonstrating similar

trends. While the literature does not suggest a "magic number" for caseloads that provide for optimum supervision, common sense certainly indicates that to achieve the stated goals of community corrections programs, caseloads must be of manageable sizes. But until agencies can point to results achieved with specified levels of resources, manageable caseload sizes will continue to be undefined and, therefore, ignored.

In *Managing Probation with Scarce Resources: Obstacles and Opportunities*, Cochran, Corbett, Nidorf, Buck, and Stiles (1991, pp. 4-5) cite two reasons for probation's vulnerability to unmanageable expansion and limited resources:

1) In many places there is not the constituency for probation that exists for prisons. "The bricks-and-mortar approach to corrections is a much more marketable item than one which concentrates on community-based interventions, particularly in a time when

conservative attitudes toward crime seem to predominate."

2) Probation overcrowding has not risen to a level for which constitutional restrictions have been imposed to set constraints on the size and operations of probation and require certain spending levels.

Clearly, community corrections cannot wait for the public or the legislature to define acceptable workloads and appropriate levels of spending. It is up to agencies themselves to state their goals, identify methods for pursuing these goals, and specify the level of human and financial resources necessary to achieve them. Until agencies begin examining performance indicators and results, however, outcome based data will be unavailable to support requests for more resources.

Maintaining a Competitive Edge

The opinions of many community corrections professionals suggest that agencies and their employees are just "trying to get by" with the limited resources they have. "Trying to get by" is not good enough in today's competition-oriented service environment. Corrections and other human service agencies are competing for limited funds from the same public coffers. As can be seen by the fiscal facts in Figure 6, corrections, and specifically probation and parole, have to struggle for what they get.

Another source of competition for community corrections agencies is privatization (Kulis, 1983). More and more states are using private agencies to effectively manage the burgeoning numbers of offenders. Private organizations are more oriented toward customer service and documenting results; their livelihood depends on it. To keep pace, community corrections agencies must begin viewing the long-term situation, properly monitoring and evaluating programs,

Figure 6 - Fiscal Facts

FACT: Compared to justice expenditures, federal, state, and local governments spent six times as much on social insurance payments, almost five times as much on national defense and international relations, four times as much on education and libraries, more than three times as much on interest on debt, twice as much on housing and the environment and almost twice as much on public welfare (Bureau of Justice Statistics [BJS], 1992).

FACT: From 1977 through 1990, the proportion of state and local government's corrections' dollars spent on institutions (including capital and operating costs) increased by 10.5 percent, while for probation, parole, and pardon services it decreased by 6.6 percent (BJS, 1992).

and communicating the findings to key stakeholders; for soon, their livelihood may also depend on it.

"Staying in business" may be the paramount rationale for adopting performance-based measures within community corrections. Everyone understands the fear of being unemployed. Not everyone (i.e., the public), however, understands the fear of being without community corrections agencies which play such a vital role in community safety. As can be seen in the remainder of this chapter, compelling reasons for performance-based measures go far beyond the mere survival of community corrections agencies. Performance-based measures provide the opportunity to demonstrate the value of community corrections' mission, activities, and accomplishments.

Measuring Short-Term
and Intermediate Outcomes

There is a high degree of consensus about the ultimate goal of any correctional program. From the perspective of taxpayers, criminal justice academicians, legislators, judges and line officers, public safety is the agreed upon bottom line. But too often an agency's impact on public safety is judged solely on *reduced recidivism*, and that bottom line becomes blurred because of the heavy burden this creates. Other factors, such as the general deterrent effects of probation/parole programs and conditions, contribute to public safety and should be included in these judgements.

It is not surprising that community corrections agencies and personnel are less than enthusiastic about recidivism measures. Recidivism is currently the primary outcome measure for community corrections, and the figures are somewhat bleak. Recidivism takes an agency from point A to point Z without much consideration of what occurs in between. It is difficult for an agency to take responsibility for, and be judged by, a single outcome. The resolution lies in two key strategies: 1) putting recidivism into perspective; and 2) measuring short-term and intermediate outcomes to more accurately assess program effectiveness.

Putting Recidivism into Perspective

> *Increasingly, the criterion of success or failure of the correctional apparatus is recidivism. It may be refined into various kinds of experience. Its definition may be specialized to meet the demands of a particular research problem. But it is the most understandable gauge...(American Correctional Association, 1966, p. 601).*

This statement reflects the situation of community corrections as well today as it did in 1966.

Recidivism, however, can be problematic as an outcome measure for several reasons.

First, numerous definitions are applied to the term "recidivism." Different definitions can produce radically different figures from the same data. Fox (1980) found that the recidivism rates for a group of parolees released from Kentucky Correctional Institutions over the period from January 1, 1974 through December 31, 1976, ranged from 13.1 percent to 37.2 percent depending upon the operational definition of recidivism that was used. Definitions of recidivism include the following:[1]

- any new arrest;

- new felony arrests only;

- any new conviction;

- new felony conviction only;

- any new commitment of sixty days or more;

- a new prison commitment only;

- new technical violations;

- a technical violation that results in incarceration;

- an arrest for the same crime;

- any arrest in which the offender was fingerprinted;

- a new arrest which resulted in incarceration of the offender;

- incarceration in a prison;

- arrest for a misdemeanor offense; and

- violent felonies.

Within the research community the debate on which definition of recidivism best represents the offender's "true" criminal activity runs deep. Many argue that "new convictions" underestimate the true level of criminal activity because of the many factors that may prevent a case from reaching a conviction including lack of evidence, failure of the court system to pursue the charge, and the failure of a jury to convict. Conversely, however, it could be argued that a "new arrest" does not substantiate that the offender committed a new crime; particularly since this nation's criminal justice system is founded on the principle of "innocent until proven guilty."

Clearly, a *standard definition* for recidivism is needed. A more realistic short-term compromise, however, would be for researchers to use multiple indicators within their studies. This would allow more meaningful interpretation of results and comparisons between studies on the common indicators used.

Second, there is tremendous variance in the amount of time involved in recidivism studies. Coupled with the numerous operational definitions of recidivism, this time variance makes it nearly impossible to compare research results. The follow-up time for recidivism studies varies from less than one year to more than six years. The length of the follow-up study impacts the interpretation of results. Research shows that a return to criminal activity is more likely to occur during the time immediately following release.

Included in the issue of time variance is that the actual time-at risk is not always taken into account in recidivism studies. In many studies, the follow-up period begins when an offender is assigned to probation or parole. Often, offenders receive a split sentence (i.e., time in jail as a condition of probation), serve time in a residential setting, or are sentenced to jail time during the period of supervision. If not factored

in, a reduction in the time-at-risk will reduce and distort the recidivism rates. To ensure that recidivism rates reveal an accurate pattern of recidivism, and to allow comparisons across studies, *standard follow-up times* should be established and *studies should account for the time-at-risk*.

One last issue related to the time frame of recidivism studies concerns whether or not community corrections should be held accountable for events (i.e., new crimes) occurring once an offender is released from supervision. In 1993, the Bureau of Justice Statistics (BJS)-Princeton Study Group concluded "...that the success of community corrections should not be based on some post program assessment of behavior" (Petersilia, 1993, p. 15).

Petersilia points out that one problem with relying primarily on recidivism is that it is a measure of post program behaviors over which community corrections has little control. She noted, "schools do not follow up their graduates to see if they slip back into ignorance or fail to hold a job after leaving school" (Petersilia, 1993, p. 14). There are many outside the educational system who feel that one measure of schools' performance *should* be how many students become employed after graduation. They also fault the educational system for failing to produce results such as graduates who can read, write, and hold down jobs that pay more than minimum wage. Categorically dismissing post program recidivism as one of several measures of outcome is tempting, but problematic. Community corrections' customers (e.g., the public) may or may not agree that there are other more important performance measures, but discounting recidivism out of hand ignores the importance of their expectations. As will be discussed more fully in the next chapter, *definitions of success must be based upon some agree-*

ment and understanding between the supplier and the end customers.

The third problem is that recidivism rates are influenced by many internal and external factors (Waldo & Griswold, 1979; Maltz & McCleary, 1977). Increased/decreased activity by law enforcement agencies or a change in judicial philosophy could have an impact on recidivism rates. A "get tough on crime/drugs" campaign will increase the number of new arrests. A new judge may want to limit formal technical violations to revokable offenses. Given either scenario, it is difficult to determine whether the change in recidivism rates was due to changes in the behavior of offenders or to changes in police/judicial actions. A related problem lies in the fact that recidivism is normally measured using only officially reported events, not self-reported or actual events. This makes recidivism rates suspect as measures of effectiveness, since they are very sensitive to policy shifts within the data-collecting agencies (Maltz & McCleary, 1977). For example, in the case of intensive supervision programs (ISP), increased recidivism rates may reflect the enhanced supervision activities and the ability to detect technical violations and/or new criminal activity. When ISP recidivism rates are compared to the recidivism rates of the standard population of offenders, the programs are labeled a failure when, in fact, the programs are doing, *in part*, what they are designed to do (i.e., increased surveillance and detection of violations).

Since other factors affect recidivism data, it is fallacious to conclude that non-recidivism demonstrates rehabilitation or success, or that recidivism demonstrates failure (Waldo & Griswold, 1979). Recidivism must be examined within the context of changes in program practices and policy shifts within the jurisdiction. Internal and external threats to validity, such as those described above, could be reduced with a *commitment to incorporating rigorous experimental*

designs into the evaluation of criminal justice innovations.

The fourth, and final problem related to recidivism as an outcome measure, is that it is always treated as a dichotomous variable. An offender is either arrested or not arrested, convicted or acquitted, a success or failure.

> *The use of recidivism as an outcome variable is replete with problems, one of which is that it is inherently limited in sensitivity by being assessed as a binary variable, as it usually is, for example, if reincarceration is the measure. A great deal of information is lost when something as complex as possible criminal activity that may or may not culminate in detection, arrest, and conviction is expressed as a simple dichotomy. Some persons engage in clear-cut criminal activity, some in borderline criminal activity, and some in no criminal activity; some persons are arrested without any hesitation, some are almost not arrested, some are almost arrested, and so on (Sechrest, White, & Brown, 1979, pp. 71-72).*

Recidivism is currently viewed as an all or nothing measure. The dichotomous measure does not allow for partial successes. If the time between positive drug tests or the number of days employed increases, is this not a partial success? If the severity of the crimes committed by an individual is reduced (e.g., from robbing banks to passing bad checks) is this not a partial success? A continuous measure of recidivism would take such factors into consideration and not judge success/failure on one single incident. *Community corrections should explore the possibility of a continuous measure for recidivism* that more accurately portrays the nature and accomplishments of the supervisory period.

The complexities of recidivism as an outcome measure suggest that its use as the primary measure of program effectiveness be revisited. While the suggested improvements for recidivism as a measure of program effectiveness (i.e., a standard definition, a standard follow-up time, accounting for time-at-risk, defining success based on some agreement between community corrections and the public, a commitment to rigorous experimental design, and the exploration of a continuous measure for recidivism) may benefit community corrections, this will only occur if recidivism is one of a number of performance-based measures. Recidivism is clearly the ultimate goal of any correctional program and cannot, therefore, be ignored. But to measure an ultimate goal in the short-term, without looking at intermediate variables and outcomes is somewhat unreasonable. The next section discusses the importance of examining performance-based measures as alternatives to recidivism.

Performance-Based Measures as Alternatives to Recidivism

John DiIulio (1992), in *Rethinking the Criminal Justice System: Toward a New Paradigm*, argued for criminal justice institutions to expand the use of outcome measures beyond crime rates and recidivism. He argued, "crime rates and recidivism are not the only, or necessarily the best, measure of what criminal justice institutions do" (p. 1). Indeed, there are numerous intermediate outcomes that more clearly gauge and illustrate the business of probation and parole. The current focus on recidivism overlooks the very activities that define the profession. Probation and parole officers provide treatment and services, conduct surveillance, and enforce court/parole board orders. By measuring the *outcomes* of these specific activities, agencies can better assess the effectiveness of various activities and program components. Furthermore, until efforts are made to disentangle these activities and components, community correc-

tions agencies will be unable to determine what it is that leads to behavioral change and a reduction in recidivism.

An example. Using the problem of substance abuse as an example, the practicality of performance-based measures becomes clear. Substance abuse is believed to be a causal factor in criminal behavior. It would make sense then, that a goal of supervision would be to reduce the level of substance abuse among the offender population. How, then, can community corrections agencies determine if this goal is being achieved? Recidivism rates alone do not provide any information about how effectively the problem of substance abuse is being addressed. Rather, the following types of research questions could guide agencies in this determination:

- What percentage of the offender population has an identified substance abuse problem?

- What percentage of these offenders were recommended for outpatient treatment? Inpatient treatment?

- What percentage of these offenders were accepted into each treatment option?
- What percentage of these offenders completed their treatment assignment?

- As measured by urinalysis, was there a difference in the level of substance abuse for offenders participating in the various treatment options?

- What was the average length of time in treatment?

Sample data and outcomes to these research questions are provided in Figure 7. A number of additional research questions could be proposed. Clearly, this information would be beneficial to an agency attempting to reduce the level of substance abuse.

Figure 7 - Treatment Outcome Flow Chart

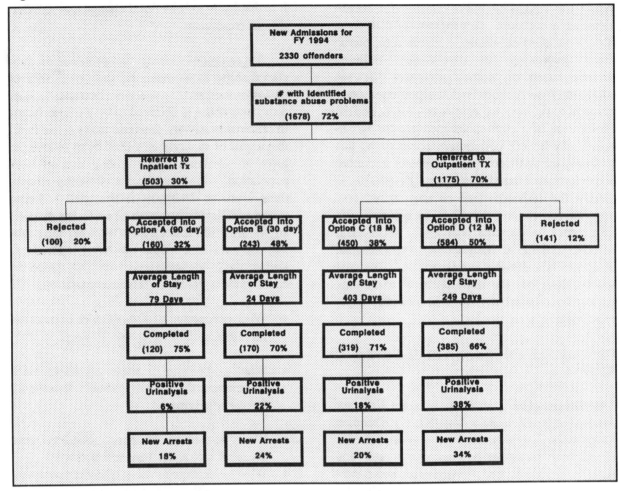

The importance of such questions becomes obvious when there is an established relationship between these factors and recidivism reduction. Several studies have revealed a positive correlation between increased participation in treatment and success on probation/parole (Anglin & Hser, 1990; Leukefeld & Tims, 1988; Jolin & Stipak, 1992; Petersilia & Turner, 1993); and a relationship between improvement in the area of substance abuse and lower rates of recidivism (Byrne & Kelly, 1989). Similar relationships exist between improvement in employment and recidivism (Byrne & Kelly, 1989; Virginia Department of Corrections, 1993) and cognitive

functioning and recidivism (Ross, Fabiano & Diemer-Ewles, 1988; Johnson & Hunter, 1992).

As these studies suggest, if these aspects of human development are changed, criminal behavior will change. Thus, by shifting the research to measure these intermediate outcomes (i.e., offender change) community corrections can begin to *assess* the effectiveness of a particular program or component, *learn* from successes, and *fine tune* these programs. Therein lies the primary value of intermediate measures; they test (confirm/reject) assumptions about different elements of the theoretical models that underlie interventions. For example, if an education program fails to reduce recidivism, was it because offenders' educational level did not improve, or was it because no employment prospects were forthcoming to match the increased levels of education, and aspirations, that were measured?

It is through this type of exploration that recidivism and other traditional measures of success can ultimately be impacted. If community corrections agencies are sincere about their intentions to control risk and address needs, a mechanism for measuring the outcomes of related activities must be developed and implemented. What an organization measures is a reflection of what they value.

The intention here is not to undermine the importance of measuring recidivism, but to suggest that, in addition, agencies begin measuring short-term, intermediate outcomes. As organizations with a mission of public safety, community corrections, like other criminal justice components, *must* be accountable for recidivism rates and play a more active role in developing and implementing policies and practices related to reduced recidivism.

The measurement of intermediate outcomes simply facilitates this role and makes recidivism rates more meaningful within the context of probation and parole activities designed to meet diverse goals. The next section offers additional rationale for using performance-based measures or to disentangle the results associated with specific program activities and components.

Cost-Benefit Analysis

In these financially stringent times, the foremost consideration of politicians and policymakers is "how much is it going to cost?" Second to that is, "is it worth it?" Community corrections

finds itself competing with incarceration for the limited correctional purse, and corrections as a whole is competing with every other publicly-funded program from education to social services. Community corrections must be able to "sell" themselves as an effective and efficient program through comprehensive and accurate cost-benefit analyses. Performance-based measures provide a framework for enhancing the value of this critical decisionmaking tool.

Since we are dealing with a finite number of dollars allocated to the criminal justice system, our direction should be toward more sophisticated front-end services. For every offender we can treat successfully in a community setting short of incarceration, we will be saving the taxpayers a considerable amount of money. [By] packaging our programs properly and using comprehensive cost analysis data...we can be successful (Schuman, 1989, p. 30).

This quote represents the primary argument used to gain support for community corrections. The problem with this is that "success" is dependent on offender rehabilitation and recidivism reduction which are both long-term endeavors, and the promised cost savings may not be immediately realized. "Programmatic overexpectation," particularly in cost-benefit terms, has been identified as one reason for program failure -- expectations are often exaggerated and cost savings and other benefits from new programs are likely to be lower than anticipated (Lewis and Greene, 1978). This is highly problematic in a governmental system where programs must prove their continued viability in the short-term. Elected officials serve terms as long as six years and as short as one year with part of their time in office spent on seeking reelection. This has led to elected officials giving their attention to matters which will produce positive, visible results in the short-term. Given these fiscal realities, it is crucial for community corrections to be able to articulate the costs and benefits of their program in the short-term. Performance-based measures enable them to do this through the use of short-term and intermediate outcome measures.

In this competitive environment in which community corrections managers work, "it is important to have a clear and precise understanding of the fiscal consequences of different choices" (McDonald, 1989, p. 1). Performance-based measures improve the accuracy of cost-benefit analysis in two key ways. First, performance-based measures provide a mechanism for incorporating performance into cost considerations. The cost of programs or services mean very little without considering how well they perform. For example, drug testing programs claim to deter drug use and lead to a savings in tax dollars and increased public safety (Office of National Drug Control Policy, 1991). Suppose, for a minute, that the up-front costs of laboratory testing are less expensive than on-site testing. Suppose further, that laboratory testing was found to be less effective than on-site testing in deterring drug use as measured by positive drug tests. If these two statements were true, the cost-savings and the value of laboratory testing would be reduced. Informed choices between various services (including those in-house) depends on knowing how well they perform as well as knowing how much they cost (McDonald, 1995). The actual cost of a service is dependent on how that service is delivered in a particular agency (McDonald, 1989).

Second, performance-based measures assist in disentangling costs and benefits within an agency.

In instances where a single agency performs a variety of different services, the costs of those services are often conflated with one another because the control of the agency's funds is more important than a precise deter-

mination of what each separate service costs. For example, probation departments typically provide both a correctional service--the supervision of offenders--and an investigative service to the court in support of the judges' sentencing function (McDonald, 1989, p. 8).

Performance-based measures provide information which allows agencies to better assess the costs and benefits of specific programs. This enhanced cost-benefit analysis will contribute to better internal decision-making -- when determining how to allocate limited funds, agencies can ascertain which services are offering "more bang for the buck" and allocate resources accordingly.

Consider the previous example of outcomes for various substance abuse treatment options within a hypothetical jurisdiction (Figure 7). As the end of the fiscal year arrives, the community corrections agency must evaluate its current contracts for services to determine the most effective use of treatment funds. The agency currently contracts with two separate service providers for a previously negotiated number of treatment slots. The decision they face is whether to keep both contracts at their current level of service or to reallocate treatment funds which could result in an increase or decrease in the service provided through each contract.

Option C, an 18 month outpatient treatment program and Option D, a 12 month outpatient treatment program, target similar populations. Once an offender is identified as appropriate for outpatient treatment, placement in Option C or D is more a matter of availability than anything else. The costs and benefits outlined in Figure 8 are simplified for the purposes here, but they portray how performance-based measures can enhance decisionmaking.

Figure 8 - Cost-Benefit Analysis of Treatment Services

	Option C	**Option D**
Cost of Service:		
Per offender	$80/month X 13.5 months (avg. length of stay) = $1080	$60/month X 8.1 months (avg. length of stay) = $480
Total cost	$1080 X 450 offenders = $486,000	$486 X 584 offenders = $283,824
Benefits of Service:	Longer involvement in treatment (403 days vs. 249 days) brings the secondary benefits of informal surveillance and risk control through structured time Lower rates of positive urinalyses (18% vs. 38%)	More offenders served Lower cost

Based on the cost information alone, Option D serves 134 more offenders for about $200,000 less and would appear to be the least costly service. However, when the benefits are examined within the context of performance the conclusion is altered. A review of performance indicators suggests that Option C is more effective in regards to treatment retention, curtailing drug use, and reducing recidivism. Each of these outcomes have societal costs and benefits that should be factored into the equation. These outcomes suggest that, in the long term, Option C may be more effective in terms of costs and benefits. As a result, the community corrections agency should consider reallocating treatment funds to increase the number of offenders receiving services through Option C. Considering that cost is such a key criteria for policymakers, it is imperative that agencies demonstrate the value of programs and services through the use of comprehensive and accurate cost-benefit data.

Cost-benefit analysis is quite complex. Its strength is in providing a framework for evaluating programs in dollar terms. It is, however, time consuming and nearly impossible to account for all benefits and costs due to the difficulty in measuring some concepts. Performance-based measures can improve cost-benefit analysis making it a more valuable decisionmaking tool. The next section discusses additional ways in which performance-based measures lead to improved management practices.

Results-Oriented Management

A 1980 report by Spectrum Analysis high-lighted important benefits of performance-based measures including: 1) an improved ability to predict and reduce recidivism; 2) assistance with goal clarification; 3) improved service delivery; 4) improved resource allocation; and 5) budgetary justification.

So why, then, are community corrections agencies resistant to measuring performance-based outcomes? The primary benefit of performance-based measures, and the primary reason agencies are hesitant to use them, are one and the same -- they put the spotlight on results and reveal hard truths about the effectiveness of probation and parole. Performance-based measures often provide information that challenges the way business is conducted and points to the need for change. This can be viewed as an organizational threat or as an opportunity for organizational growth. This section will explore the latter -- ways in which agencies can benefit from applying techniques which distinguish success from failure.

In a 1993 national best seller, *Reinventing Government*, Osborne and Gaebler propose a change in the way governments and governmental agencies do business. They recommend a "results-oriented government" based on the following seven principles:

1) What gets measured gets done;
2) If you don't measure results, you can't tell success from failure;
3) If you can't see success, you can't reward it;
4) If you can't reward success, you're probably rewarding failure;
5) If you can't see success, you can't learn from it;
6) If you can't recognize failure, you can't correct it; and
7) If you can demonstrate results, you can win public support.

A discussion about each of these principles and specific examples of how they apply to community corrections follows.

What gets measured gets done. "In large organizations, public and private, things are counted, and whatever is counted, counts" (Osborne &

Gaebler, 1993, p. 147). The best example of this phenomenon within community corrections is the current practice of counting the number and type of supervision contacts. Based on an offender's level of risk, an officer must conduct a pre-determined number of contacts. Often, a primary focus of case audits is whether or not an officer is in compliance with contact standards. Because an officer's performance is measured by this standard, the contact or activity, rather than the outcome becomes the focus of supervision. This is problematic for several reasons, which are discussed in the principles that follow.

If you don't measure results, you can't tell success from failure. To depict the problematic nature of counting activities rather than results, the data in Tables 1 and 2 have been compiled to determine if employment objectives are being met. Studies have revealed a positive correlation between improvement in employment and success on probation and parole (Byrne & Kelly, 1989; Virginia Department of Corrections, 1993), making this an appropriate example for reiterating the importance of measuring intermediate outcomes. Table 1 shows data gathered in an agency that counts activities, in this case referrals, as the primary means for assessing officer performance. Table 2 shows data gathered in an agency that measures results.

What information does the data within these two tables provide? Both tables provide information regarding the number of offenders with needs in the area of employment per caseload. Table 1 suggests that some officers make more employment referrals than others. Based on this information it would appear that Officer Jones' performance exceeds that of his co-workers because of the higher percentage of referrals for unemployed offenders. What it does not say is that Officer Jones refers all unemployed offenders to the same employment program regardless of their individual needs; that he does not follow-up on the referral; or that he does not assist

Table 1 - Counting Activities

OFFICER	# OF UNEMPLOYED OFFENDERS AT INITIAL ASSESSMENT	# OF REFERRALS
Smith	43	32 (74%)
Jones	22	20 (91%)
Larson	35	25 (71%)
Thomas	38	30 (79%)
Wilson	28	22 (79%)

Table 2 - Measuring Results

OFFICER	# OF UNEMPLOYED OFFENDERS AT INITIAL ASSESSMENT	% OBTAINING EMPLOY-MENT WITHIN SIX MONTHS
Smith	43	24 (56%)
Jones	22	5 (23%)
Larson	35	25 (71%)
Thomas	38	24 (63%)
Wilson	28	14 (50%)

or monitor offenders in their job seeking efforts. Nor does it tell the true story -- that only 20 percent of Officer Jones' unemployed offenders obtained employment during the first six months as opposed to 50-70 percent of his co-workers' unemployed offenders. As can be seen by this example, the practice of counting activities rather than results is misleading. It can conceal poor officer performance and organizational deficiencies.

If you can't see success, you can't reward it. Regardless of Officer Jones' shortcomings, and regardless of the fact that only 20 percent of the unemployed offenders on his caseload obtained employment during the first six months, he receives praise for his work with unemployed offenders, based upon the data reported in Table 1. Meanwhile, his co-workers do not receive credit for the more positive outcomes achieved with their unemployed offenders, because *results* aren't measured.

Employees are motivated by internal incentives (e.g., a sense of accomplishment, pride) and external incentives (i.e., career advancement, praise, a monetary reward). The internal incentives generally develop after receiving external incentives. Therefore, it is important that external incentives are provided and that they target the appropriate behavior. The establishment of specific performance standards will assist in this regard. An example of a performance standard related to the goal of offender employment may be "50 percent of unemployed offenders will obtain employment during their first six months of supervision." The information in Table 2 provides for the establishment of realistic and achievable performance standards.

If you can't reward success, you're probably rewarding failure. By rewarding false successes, as in the case of Officer Jones, managers may inadvertently promote undesirable performance. Without a means to differentiate success from failure, decisions regarding performance reviews, program continuation or program expansion become little more than subjective judgement calls. "The majority of legislators and public executives have no idea which programs they fund are successful and which are failing. When they cut budgets, they have no idea whether they are cutting muscle or fat. Lacking objective information on outcomes, they make their decisions largely on political considerations" (Osborne & Gaebler, 1993, p. 147). By measuring results and communicating successes, community corrections can begin encouraging desired officer performance and protecting themselves from political whims.

If you can't see success, you can't learn from it. While Table 2 might not provide enough information either, it tells a more meaningful story. A review of the data in Table 2 would provide a unit supervisor with enough information to begin asking important questions such as:

- What contributes to Officer Larson's success in achieving employment objectives?

- Do the caseload characteristics differ among officers (e.g., is his caseload comprised of offenders with more skills and experience)?

- What factors does Officer Larson consider when making referrals to community resources?

- What techniques does Officer Larson use when working with offenders on employment objectives?

By establishing formal benchmarks, or performance standards, associated with specific practices, and measuring results, successful programs/practices can be identified and expanded. This systematic approach to improving agency operations will lead to community corrections being viewed as a learning organization committed to goal attainment.

If you can't recognize failure, you can't correct it. The benefit of recognizing failure lies in the ability to correct it, rather than to admonish it. In the example above, measuring employment outcomes provided a basis for further exploration; a chance to improve organizational effectiveness. By examining Officer Larson's practices as they relate to facilitating offender employment, the practices of other officers and the agency as a whole can be modified and improved.

Without effective processes for program monitoring and evaluation, and valid outcome measures, the reason(s) for program failure are difficult to trace. If the failed program component(s) cannot be identified, the situation cannot be corrected and the entire program will be labeled a failure. The classic example of this is the research on intensive supervision programs (ISP). The Bureau of Justice Assistance (BJA) sponsored an intensive supervision project that involved 2,000 offenders, fourteen programs, and nine states. An evaluation conducted by the RAND Corporation (Petersilia & Turner, 1993) concluded that the ISP programs were not successful in reducing recidivism rates. In fact, in eleven sites the arrest rates were higher for ISP participants than for the control group. Recidivism was the primary outcome measure, and inputs such as the number of contacts and drug tests conducted were tracked. Because the programs were evaluated as an entire package, it was difficult to disentangle the effects that various program components and practices had on recidivism rates. The entire programs were labeled a failure when, in all likelihood, many practices may have produced positive results and others negative. Had mechanisms for distinguishing success from failure been in place, minor program improvements may have resulted in more positive outcomes.

If you can demonstrate results, you can win public support. If community corrections agencies can demonstrate that they are meeting agency goals and objectives, they are more likely to win the support of the general public and other interested stakeholders. If a program has public support it is more likely to receive the state and federal funding that it needs to continue and/or expand its operations.

In the above example, the agency is able to demonstrate that offender employment rates can be increased with appropriate resources and supervision techniques. This outcome data may be useful in securing the financial and human resources to train other officers on the skills related to facilitating offender employment. It could also provide potent justification for expanding employment services for offenders, especially if the agency can point to reductions in recidivism for those offenders who show improvements in the area of employment. Within this scenario, effective communication is imperative to adequately represent the program's benefits for offenders, agencies and communities.

Communicating What Community Corrections Does

It is the responsibility of community corrections agencies and personnel to clarify their values, goals and objectives and to collect and report data through which they are accurately represented. Only through demonstrating results can community corrections expect to impact the public opinion that is so influential to policymaking and justify human and financial resources.

Crime is the number one concern for American citizens. Front page newspaper headlines and top news stories often concern a specific heinous crime or crime rates in general. Political campaigns are won and lost because of a position on crime. This focus on crime, and the impact it can have on the policies and practices of community corrections, suggests that communicating agency benefits and accomplishments is essential. In order for community corrections to effectively communicate what it does, agencies must improve their institutional capacity to prove their program's impacts. Establishing performance-based measures is a good starting point.

The types of things counted and reported send a strong message about the values and aims of an agency. If someone unfamiliar with community corrections were to examine the things currently counted (i.e., contacts, the number of drug tests conducted, the number of offenders on electronic monitoring or house arrest, and technical violations) they could reasonably conclude that the purpose of community corrections is to "watch and catch" offenders. A further examination of the rates of new arrests could lead to another reasonable conclusion -- community corrections is not very good at "watching and catching."

If, however, an agency counted and reported that during fiscal year 1995:

- 82 percent of victim restitution ordered was successfully collected and distributed to victims;

- 78 percent of victims expressed satisfaction with probation/parole victim services;

- 90 percent of the offenders without a high school diploma earned a GED;

- 85 percent of all offenders were gainfully employed;

- 75 percent of offenders with an identified substance abuse problem successfully completed an approved treatment program;

- there was a 32 percent reduction in the number of positive urinalyses for offenders identified as having a drug problem; and

- the average reduction in the level of offender risk, as measured by a six month reassessment, was 12 percent,

that same individual could reasonably conclude that the agency is concerned about the rights of crime victims and facilitating behavioral change in offenders, and that the agency produces positive outcomes in these areas.

Ongoing System of Monitoring and Evaluation

The final rationale for performance-based measures concerns the need for an ongoing system of monitoring and evaluation. The value of large scale evaluations or studies cannot be understated. However, they require a great deal of time and expense and only provide outcomes for a specified period of time. Performance-based measures provide agencies with organizational feedback that drives program improvements and are a continuous process for monitoring and evaluation as opposed to a single point-in-time assessment.

Specific performance-based measurements provide a systematic method for collecting and reporting data that document community corrections' value. They make probation and parole outcomes tangible. By focusing on outcomes specifically linked to program components, interventions and behavioral change, conclusions can be drawn about which aspects of the programs lead to the ultimate goals of any correctional program: reduced recidivism and increased public safety.

Conclusion

As can be seen, performance-based measures offer many advantages.

- They provide tangible support for human and financial resource requests allowing community corrections to successfully compete for limited public funds.

- They help to put recidivism into perspective by measuring short-term and intermediate outcomes that provide a better assessment of the activities that define the profession (e.g., treatment and services, surveillance, enforcement), and more clearly depict what community corrections does and how well they do it.

- They provide information about which programmatic aspects lead to the ultimate goals of reduced recidivism and public safety.

- They enhance the value of cost-benefit analysis by incorporating performance into cost considerations and by demonstrating the short-term costs and benefits of specific programs and services;

- They enable agencies to practice "results-oriented management" by establishing benchmarks and standards, distinguishing success from failure, and providing a basis for organizational improvements.

• They create a learning environment and contribute to organizational growth.

• They articulate organizational values and demonstrate a commitment to achieving results.

• They provide structured organizational feedback and a continuous process for monitoring and evaluation.

• They empower community corrections agencies by arming them with information and the capacity to demonstrate their value.

How then, can an agency establish a system of performance-based measures? The next chapter will describe a model for performance-based measurement. The model is designed to assist agencies in developing and implementing performance-based measures that more accurately assess an agency's accomplishments and provide a basis for systematic and ongoing organizational improvements.

---

[1] An extensive review of correctional evaluations revealed these diverse definitions of recidivism. Please see: Boone, H. N. (1994, Winter). An examination of recidivism and other outcome measures: A review of the literature. *Perspectives, 18*(1), 12-18.

CHAPTER TWO

DEVELOPING AN AGENCY-SPECIFIC PERFORMANCE-BASED EVALUATION STRATEGY

Introduction

The advantages of performance-based measures are clear. The process for developing them, however, can be quite complex. Performance-based measures provide internal and external feedback at the policy, program, and staff levels about the relationships between practices, objectives, and results. Additionally, they reflect decisions about the business of community corrections, who the customers are, what they want, and how their needs will be met and determined. To the degree that performance measures are not integrated as part of standard business practices, the feedback will be less credible, less useful, and can even be contrary to an organization's objectives.

Figure 9 - A Model for Developing Performance-Based Measures

The purpose of this chapter is to provide a framework for developing agency-specific performance-based measures. It introduces a

model to assist community corrections agencies in identifying alternative outcome measures and in establishing a performance-based measurement strategy (Figure 9). The development of a comprehensive performance-based measurement strategy requires the examination (or development) of the following:

• values inherent in the agency/program;

• an agency mission statement;

• goals of the agency/program;

• activities performed to accomplish the goals; and

• measures for determining how well the activities are being performed and what impact they are having.

Alignment of these key organizational practices enhances an agency's chances for achieving desired results.

This chapter will discuss the complexities of performance-based measurement, and demonstrate the model's utility for developing such a system within community corrections agencies.

Implementing the Model - Starting at the Beginning With the End in Mind

In any developmental process, there is a tendency to want to bypass the first several steps and proceed directly to implementation. In her article, *Conditions that Permit Intensive Supervision Programs to Survive*, Petersilia (1990) states "research on innovation and change suggest that how a program is developed and instituted affects its survival as much or more than its content does" (p. 127). This same principle applies to the development of a performance-based measurement strategy.

It would be very simple for someone in the organization to develop a list of alternative outcome measures, to write a memo instructing personnel to begin collecting the data, and to pass judgement on an agency and its personnel on the basis of these measures. Until, of course, dissension arises. Staff and organizations will resist performance measures because such measures are threatening and represent change. Evaluation, in any form, can be discomforting. After the fact, favorable evaluations are warmly received, but few see negative feedback as an opportunity to learn.

Involving a representative cross-section of staff in selecting process and outcome measures helps in several ways. For example, it increases organizational learning regarding the trade-offs involved in measuring performance. Is it, for example, more important to measure the number of contacts or to evaluate what happened during the contacts? Staff input increases buy-in, and decreases normal fears and resistance to evaluation.

Of critical significance is the involvement of line personnel and supervisors in this developmental process. It is line officers who are responsible for performing the activities designed to achieve organizational goals and the supervisors who must assess this performance. Their input and buy-in is essential. Involving line staff can change their perceptions of this process from one that is threatening to one that offers opportunity. By inviting, *and valuing*, officer input, agencies can identify process and outcome measures that truly reflect their values, mission, goals and accomplishments. A performance-based measurement system that provides officers

Figure 10 - Focus Groups

Focus Groups:
A Strategy for Involving Key Stakeholders

Focus groups are one-time meetings with various groups of stakeholders. A structured question/answer format is used for gathering information. Following are steps for conducting effective focus groups:

1. Select an internal or external consultant, who is unbiased and non-threatening, to facilitate the focus groups.

2. Establish groups consisting of cohorts of individuals that encourage open and honest communication and provide a true representation of the organization (e.g., line officers, unit supervisors, agency administrators, judges, legislators).

3. Identifying several key questions that will be asked of each group to elicit the desired information.

4. Convene focus groups:

   -- inform participants of the purpose of the focus groups;
   -- ask key questions;
   -- probe for additional information as needed and encourage participation from all members of the group; and
   -- record all answers to each of the key questions without identifying individual responses.

5. Compile answers from all focus groups into a report and provide it to all participants and other members of the organization who will be affected by the proposed changes.

with information and feedback on matters important to them will gain their commitment to the necessary practices of data collection and data compilation. Most importantly, it will gain their commitment to the results.

Figure 11 - Guiding Stakeholder Input

Critical Questions
• What are the primary goals of the agency/program? • What activities are conducted to achieve these goals? • What is the theoretical basis for program activities? • What is currently measured to demonstrate the success/failure of these activities or the overall agency/ program? • What perceptions are there about current measurements of program success/failure? • What measurements would be a fair test of agency/program operations? Staff performance? • What resources are needed to implement these measures?

Making time for a thorough developmental phase can have many positive effects in addition to promoting stakeholder buy-in. Examining such issues often creates questions in the minds of many -- what is the basic theory, or philosophy, upon which probation and parole activities are based? Are the activities conducted in support of this philosophy? Do the things currently counted reflect that philosophy? Too often, because of the reactive posture of current operations, these questions are not considered. Many agencies, while stating that they are in the business of behavioral change, do nothing to measure whether that change has occurred. Many are concerned about being judged solely

on the basis of recidivism, yet rates of new arrests and technical violations are the only things consistently counted and reported. Asking and answering such questions, while time consuming, can clarify an agency's values, mission, and methods. It can be enlightening and can promote a renewed sense of understanding and commitment.

Figures 10 and 11 offer a strategy and critical questions for guiding stakeholder input and initiating the development of an agency-specific performance-based measurement strategy. The next sections will discuss the importance of exploring and developing each model component (i.e., values, mission, goals, activities and measures).

Clarifying Values

Figure 12 - Step 1: Clarifying Values

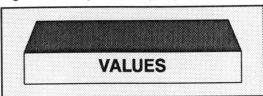

Values are "principles, standards, or qualities considered worthwhile" (American Heritage Dictionary, Second College Edition) and represent an organization's fundamental beliefs upon which agency practices are based. The first, and perhaps most critical, step in developing a performance-based strategy is to clarify and communicate agency values. Values shape decisions, actions, and consequently, results, for individuals and organizations. While outcomes, or results, that are measured reflect an organization's values, it is not the same thing as *valuing, or committing,* to the process which gets the result. A hypothetical probation agency might have a mission statement, "to provide quality supervision to all offenders," but if that organization does not really *value* quality it will not be practiced (or recognized), much less measured.

Value statements serve as the motivating force behind agency policies and practices, from hiring officers, to the case supervision of offenders, to monitoring and evaluation. Figure 13 lists the values of the Maricopa County Adult Probation Department in Phoenix, Arizona (Maricopa County Adult Probation Department, 1993).

Figure 13 - Agency Values - Maricopa County Adult Probation Department

- We believe that individuals can change and that we can be instrumental in directing that change.

- We believe in being sensitive to the needs of victims of crime.

- We believe in promoting and maintaining a positive, safe, and healthy work environment.

These value statements are reflected within all organizational levels of the Maricopa County Adult Probation Department. The administration demonstrates their commitment to these values by allocating financial and human resources to extensive officer training in behavioral change techniques and officer safety, and to the development of a comprehensive continuum of services designed to address offender needs. Unit supervisors and line officers demonstrate their commitment to these values through the application of problem-solving approaches to case super-vision, high rates of restitution collection and the coordination and delivery of Victim Impact Panels.

Figure 14 lists the values of the Georgia Department of Corrections (Georgia Department of

Figure 14 - Agency Values - Georgia Department of Corrections

- It is our duty to be truly accountable to ourselves and the public for the effective and efficient use of our time and all available resources to accomplish our mission.

- We are responsible for providing offenders a broad range of services and programs according to their individual needs and the risk they pose to our staff and the community.

Corrections, 1993). Georgia Department of Corrections' commitment to accountability is demonstrated by their comprehensive evaluation unit and ongoing monitoring and evaluation activities. The second value statement is reflected in a thorough risk/need assessment process, and the development of a continuum of services and sanctions designed to meet the diverse risks and needs of offenders.

Establishing and articulating values conveys a positive identity and promotes an under-standing about the beliefs and priorities of an organization to both internal and external stakeholders. While values, themselves, are not measurable, measuring related processes and outcomes demonstrates a sincerity and commitment to the value.

Defining a Mission

Mission statements set forth, in broad language, the organization's ultimate purpose. They clarify an organization's strategic intent, its reason for being. Stephen Covey (1991) talks about beginning with the end in mind. Petersilia (1993) believes that "a necessary first step toward developing performance indicators is to articulate the organization's mission..." (p. 6).

Figure 15 - Step 2: Defining a Mission

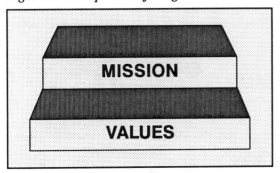

Corrections agencies, however, often lack clear missions (Petersilia, 1993; Markley, 1989), leading to serious organizational repercussions. Confusion about the business of an organization is commonly associated with reactive management, confused operations, and ineffective services. Therefore, the second critical step in developing a performance-based measurement strategy is to develop a mission statement that reflects the organization's values and its strategic intent.

Mission statements seem frivolous when they are not linked to operations. Frequently the chief administrators or a small group of individuals, none of whom are line personnel, quickly draft a flowery statement intended to impress. Sometimes the statement is hung on the wall or sometimes it is put in a departmental manual, but nowhere does it steer planning and operations toward desired outcomes.

A mission statement should clarify organizational intent -- e.g., "protect the community," without spelling out how it will be done -- e.g., "through electronic monitoring." APPA's Issues Development Committee recently defined the following essential elements in mission development.

Initiative and involvement of top leadership. The initiative and support of top leadership is essential to developing and operationalizing a meaningful mission. However, the agency mission should not simply mirror an administrator's goals.

Broad-based involvement of staff in the development process. The process of developing a useful (otherwise, why bother) mission statement is as important as the end product itself. Involving staff in the development of an agency mission clarifies the purpose(s) of community corrections and promotes buy-in. Staff can then develop and implement methods with the intent of achieving the organization's mission.

Broadly stated. Imbedded within the mission is a set of implicit or explicit values. NASA's famous mission, "to put a man on the moon by...," was clear and broadly stated. It implied the value of space exploration and science; it did not specify how that mission was going to be achieved.

Achievable. NASA's mission was believed to be achievable. Defining a mission that is not reasonably achievable -- "to eliminate crime" -- sets the stage for almost certain failure. At the other extreme, a mission that sets forth minimal expectations would not be very inspiring.

Considers customers and stakeholders. Community corrections agencies exist to provide products or services which satisfy the needs of customers. An agency that defines a mission which ignores or is contrary to the needs of its customers will be short-lived.

Linked to methods of achieving goals. Missions should guide operations and performance measures. Methods that contradict or fail to support the mission of an organization will produce unintended results.

Periodic review. Missions, customers' expectations, and external and internal conditions change. A common practice in community corrections is reference to missions which no longer reflect the agency's interests or those of their customers.

Figure 16 - Sample Mission Statements

> The mission of the **Maricopa County Adult Probation Department** is to provide information to the court and provide community-based sanctions for adult offenders. This is accomplished by conducting investigations, enforcing court orders, and providing treatment opportunities.
>
> The mission of the **Georgia Department of Corrections** is to protect the public and staff by managing offenders either in a safe and secure environment or through effective community supervision according to their needs and risks. In collaboration with the community and other agencies, we provide programs which offer offenders the opportunity to become responsible and productive law-abiding citizens.

The inclusive development of an achievable, yet inspirational, mission statement can be a long and involved process. The end result, however, is worth the expenditure of time; a strong mission promotes organizational cohesiveness and increases overall effectiveness.

Clarifying Organizational Goals

A broadly stated mission, while desirable, can be overwhelming. A key question is left unanswered -- how does the agency get there? The next step in developing a performance-based measurement strategy, clarifying organizational goals, begins to answer this question by bringing the mission into focus and breaking it down into manageable, achievable components.

For example, Figure 18 includes the goals of the Maricopa County Adult Probation Department. As shown by this example, program goals map out the future and provide a measure of success.

Figure 17 - Step 3: Clarifying Organizational Goals

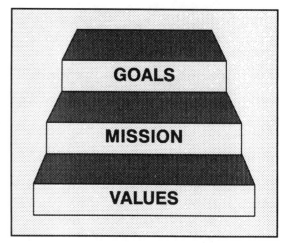

They specify the intentions of the agency and direct organizational activities.

The importance of goal clarification cannot be overstated. Goals that are overly ambitious or conflicting can create organizational confusion; one goal may be achieved at the expense of another. Intensive Supervision Programs (ISPs) have encountered this problem. The goals of many ISPs include increased public protection, rehabilitation of the offender, the provision of an intermediate punishment, a reduction in prison crowding, *and* a cost savings (Clear & Hardyman, 1990; Tonry, 1990). Trying to be everything to everyone has created a no-win situation for ISPs and many other community corrections programs. For example, the more stringently ISPs impose the punitive conditions (as a means of providing an intermediate punishment and increasing public protection), the more likely they are to exacerbate prison crowding and to approach the costs of imprisonment (Turner & Petersilia, 1992). Furthermore, the claim of reduced costs underestimates the increased level of staffing required, surveillance costs (i.e., equipment), and the expansion of social service resources needed to achieve the rehabilitative aims (Cochran, 1989). This type of scenario

Figure 18 - Organizational Goals - Maricopa County Adult Probation Department

- To conduct complete and thorough investigations and provide the court with accurate, objective information and professional evaluations and recommendations.

- To secure treatment resources for probationers.

- To assist probationers to remain in the community through appropriate intervention and supervision.

- To assess the behavior of probationers and bring to the court's attention those offenders who are in serious noncompliance with court orders.

- To foster professional development, safety, and well-being of staff.

- To set direction consistent with the department's mission and values.

threatens organizational credibility and causes people to question the true value and purpose of community corrections programs.

One solution to this problem may lie in specifying and differentiating short- and long-term goals. For example, incapacitative and specific deterrent conditions may have an immediate, short-range focus that provides in-program crime control, whereas rehabilitation has been associated with long-term behavioral change (Harland & Rosen, 1987). As discussed in Chapter One, recidivism is a long-term, *ultimate* goal that is often measured in the short-term. By specifying that recidivism is a long-term goal, which is supported by short-term goals such as enforcing court orders and securing treatment resources for offenders, agencies can clarify their intentions and guide agency operations toward immediate and ultimate goal achievement.

Selecting Activities that Support Organizational Goals

Figure 19 - Step 4: Selecting Activities that Support Organizational Goals

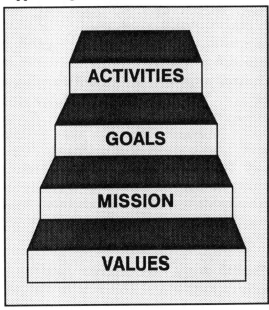

Various methods of supervision are used to achieve the goals of community corrections. Selecting methods, or activities, that support an agency's stated goals is the next step in developing an agency-specific performance-based measurement strategy.

Supervision methods are generally discussed in terms of assistance versus authority; social work versus law enforcement. The role of community corrections has vacillated between these points since its inception. The purpose here is not to advocate one method or orientation over the other, but to encourage agencies to examine their organizational philosophies and selected methods of supervision within the context of established goals. Chances are, this examination will lead to an integration of both roles and methods.

Authoritative supervision methods are those focused on control, monitoring, and surveillance and are most often associated with those agencies and officers having a law-enforcement orientation. Supervision tools such as curfews, house arrest, electronic monitoring, urine screens, and frequent office, home and employment visits are all examples of authoritative supervision methods. They are specifically designed to monitor and control the offender's behavior. Assistance is associated with service provision, either directly or through advocacy and/or brokerage. Activities include employment counseling, problem solving, and educating. The focus of these activities is on rehabilitation; showing the offender an alternative to a criminal lifestyle. Agencies and officers emphasizing the role of assistance are identified as having a social work orientation.

Though theory may separate authority and assistance into an opposable dichotomy, research has indicated, and observation of probation/parole practices has shown, that officers do not necessarily operate in this manner, and *can* employ both methods as they feel necessary to supervise the offenders on their caseloads (Clear & Latessa, 1993; Erwin & Bennett, 1987). The following quote illustrates the decisions officers face when dealing with offenders.

> *The search for role development in probation and parole supervision has been demonstrated by a few themes. One is that the probation/parole officer faces a series of expectations that do not always fit together well. Especially, there is a conflict between expectations that the officer will respond to the offender's needs, but will also hold the offender accountable to the legal system's requirements... There seems to be a common assumption that probation and parole officers cannot be both the source of service and the agent of control for offenders without serious mixed messages and confusion for the client*

and the officer. Yet measures of officers' preference for these two role orientations consistently show that some officers score high on both, some on neither (Clear & Latessa, 1993, p. 14).

This separation of roles seems to be perpetuated by the organizational philosophy and values rather than because of officers' inability to integrate roles (Clear & Latessa, 1993). The punitive ideology associated with corrections over the past 15-20 years has led to a focus on authoritative and control-oriented methods. Harris (1987) notes that this emphasis on control has caused probation and parole agents to focus on technology designed to detect violations, such as urinalysis and electronic monitoring, which leads to an adversarial relationship with offenders. Others have lamented the dependency on electronic means for controlling offenders, cautioning that probation/parole officers could lose their professionalism to the electronic monitor, becoming experts at monitoring systems rather than supervision (Erwin, 1990; Corbett, 1989). On the other hand, the social work/assistance orientation has been criticized for emphasizing rehabilitation and the needs of the offender over community safety. Agencies and officers with this orientation have been accused of "coddling" offenders.

Viewing offender supervision as a series of demands in direct opposition to one another does nothing to advance public safety or offender rehabilitation. The facts are that both offenders and the community are valuable; and that both assistance and authority are effective supervision tools when utilized appropriately. These need not be either/or propositions.

The primary value of performance-based measurements is that they assist agencies in determining which activities do, in fact, lead to goal achievement. Results-oriented data removes the debate from one of preferred style or orientation to one of "what works." Selected activities will change as agencies enhance their knowledge and understanding of what activities are effective.

Identifying Performance-Based Measures

Figure 20 - Step 5: Identifying Performance-Based Measurements

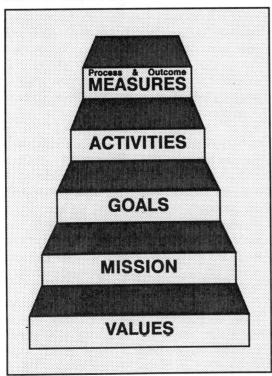

The in-depth exploration of agency values, mission, goals, and activities, as described in steps 1-4 of APPA's model for performance-based measurement, provides a solid foundation for a measurement strategy that assesses and communicates what an agency does and how well they do it. Petersilia (1993) has stated, "once the agency has identified its goals and the methods it uses to address each goal, it can specify objective (measurable) criteria that determines the extent to which the activities are being performed" (p. 8). The remainder of this chapter will be devoted to step 5 of the model, the identification of agency-specific measures.

Because of the complexities involved, discussions are in order regarding:

* the difference between process and outcome measures and the importance of developing both; and

* the relationship between processes, outcomes and community corrections customers.

Distinguishing Between Processes and Outcomes

Performance measurement in community corrections has been a case of confusion and extremes. At one extreme are measures that focus solely on the *process, or activities,* used to achieve an outcome. At the other extreme, effectiveness has been based solely on *ultimate outcomes* such as recidivism. Trying to sort the extremes can be difficult and confusing. *In reality, both process and outcome measures are necessary.*

Process measures are needed to determine if a program was implemented as designed. Specifically, they provide a mechanism to: identify program goals; consider causal linkages to criminal behavior; specify the program's target population; describe what services are actually being delivered; investigate unanticipated consequences; and search for explanations of success, failure and change (Harris, 1991). Process measures may include the number and type of contacts, the number of referrals for treatment, the style of interaction between officers and offenders, or the extent to which offenders were appropriately classified. Processes can be examined through observation of program activities, interviews and case audits (Harris, 1991).

Outcome measures are needed to assess a program's impact. As discussed in the previous chapter, multiple intermediate outcomes should be measured in addition to recidivism. "Because recidivism-centered findings provide administrators with no direction for program improvement, they are routinely pushed aside with no corrective actions taken" (Harris, 1991, p. 9). Outcome measures that more effectively guide program improvements may include rates of offender employment, reduced drug abuse or a reduction in risk levels. Various research methods can be employed to assess a program's impact. These are discussed in *Appendix A, An Administrators Guide to Evaluation*. Within the context of this monograph, the focus is on tracking and descriptively reporting outcomes, or program results, on an ongoing basis.

If only outcomes are examined, little direction is available for program policymaking (Harris, 1991). Examining processes, however, helps to explain why such effects were produced, and how practices can be modified to produce desired outcomes (Blalock, 1990). By controlling processes, agencies can control outcomes. Demming (1986) stated that as much as 85 percent of undesirable results are associated with any process controllable by management, while fifteen percent can be attributed to individuals. Organizations seeking to prioritize how they spend their evaluation resources should address process measures first to obtain fundamental feedback on whether services are being delivered according to specifications. If the feedback confirms that processes are meeting agency targets, *then* questions about outcomes are meaningful.

The importance of accurately distinguishing between these types of measures cannot be understated. Take the case of Datapoint, a computer manufacturing firm (see Figure 21).

The real world experience of this company illustrates a number of key points:

- Don't confuse process measures (e.g., the number of contracts written) with outcome measures (e.g., did we make a profit?).

Figure 21 - Datapoint

To monitor the performance of their sales staff, Datapoint Management selected and routinely tracked total sales for each salesperson. They also wanted to provide incentives linked to performance measures. Since the company was in the business of manufacturing computers to sell, they decided to pay the sales force based on total sales. Total sales was defined, reported, and measured as the total dollar amount of sales contracts written by each salesperson. Sales of the company's computers quickly exceeded all expectations, and the factory couldn't keep up with the demand. Naive external investors based their decisions on the company's internal performance data and quickly grabbed up the company's stock! Subsequent audits and investigations, however, told a different story about the company's performance. The performance of the company's sales force, and consequently their compensation, was measured by the face value of customers' purchase orders rather than cash receipts. The other problem was that the company had a thirty day "return with no questions asked" policy. The highly motivated sales force naturally emphasized the lenient contract cancellation features as an incentive to customers. Many customers canceled their orders, but because management was measuring sales and not cancellations, feedback to manufacturing increased production instead of decreasing it. Unsold computers began to stack up. Sales people, who had become accustomed to large commissions, rented secret warehouses to store the returns. During an external audit some salespersons loaded unsold computers into rented trucks and drove them around the city's beltway to avoid detection.

- Process and outcome measures are at best subject to the "garbage in -- garbage out" principle.

- Upstream choices and applications of process measures have downstream impacts on outcomes.

- Performance measures represent, but are not always the same as, actual performance.

- To be useful to those inside or outside an organization, measures must be part of an overall strategy designed to enhance clearly defined objectives.

Relating Processes and Outcomes to Customers

Identification of external and internal customers helps in making the important distinction between measuring results and measuring the process of attaining results. Organizations exist to satisfy external consumers of their products or services. Rose Washington, former Commissioner of New York's Department of Juvenile Justice told her staff at Spofford, "this place is managed like a corporation, like IBM or Proctor & Gamble, and these children are our product" (Good, 1993). Historically, public sector funding has:

> seldom, if ever..[been] tied to performance. Yet it is clear that employees should be paid for what they earn, not for what they need or believe they deserve. They must be paid for satisfying the customer (McClendon, 1992, p. 111).

Customer service, however is a different and more difficult concept in the public sector. Probation and parole exist within a context of courts, politicians, and the public -- each with different expectations and needs. A fundamental difference between customer service in the private and public sectors is choice. Community corrections does not have total freedom to choose their customers or the number to be served. Thus "customers" are often viewed more as "consumers" which changes the nature of service delivery. As Total Quality Management (TQM) initiatives and "reinvention of government" became popular, however, so did the awareness that public organizations have

both internal and external customers, as well as suppliers (Osborne & Gaebler, 1993). Hence, customer satisfaction is being introduced as a key objective for community corrections.

No organization can be all things to all people. One way to sort out the confusion is to clarify and prioritize the organization's external customers (i.e., who receives the organization's outputs?). The process of customer identification can be simple or complex. A simple two stage process, such as the one illustrated in Table 3, is more than adequate for most public sector organizations. In Stage I, all possible customers are identified. In Stage II, customers are separated into internal and external customers according to the type of intended output. In this hypothetical example, line staff complete presentence investigations primarily for the judge and legislature who are their external customers, but also for their internal customers, the chief and supervision officers. Prioritizing customers can be based on one or more criteria such as frequency of interaction, or how critical they are to an organization's survival.

Customers and their relative priority are context and output specific. Key questions when going through this process are: What is the objective? And, who is the service or program intended to satisfy? The answers to these questions are important as agencies plan and evaluate programs and services.

As Figure 22 shows, each process may be part of a larger process, with discrete or overlapping sets of suppliers and customers. For example, a presentence investigation process may use interviews, investigations and report writing to produce and supply an output (i.e., a presentence report) needed by an internal customer (i.e., the supervision program). The presentence report then becomes an input to the supervision process which supplies outputs to external customers (i.e., the public), intended to produce

Table 3 - Two Stages of Customer Identification

I. Identified	II. Grouped and prioritized by output	
<u>All Customers</u>	<u>Presentence Investigation</u>	
Budget office Legislature Judges The Chief Supervisor Public Law enforcement Supervision officers	<u>Internal</u> 1. Manager 2. The Chief 3. Officers	<u>External</u> 1. Judges 2. Legislature (Public?)

decreased assaultive behavior in offenders. If the judge is viewed as the primary customer of the presentence process, however, the relationships change.

In summary, suppliers receive and employ "inputs," such as people, equipment, materials and offenders, which are combined into processes designed to produce outputs for one or more end users or customers. One purpose of performance-based measures is to be able to increase the understanding of relationships between customers, processes and outcomes.

Need for Structural and Technological Changes

Once an organizational framework has been developed for performance-based measurement, it must be supported by structural changes and technological advances. Agencies need to consider the following questions when developing their performance-based measurement strategy:

• What changes must take place in the organization to allow for effective performance review?

• Who is assigned the duties (e.g., at what level; in what job descriptions)?

What are the consequences of performance review (e.g., how do we insure that the results mean anything, or that anything will be done with the findings)?

Structural Changes

Downward Movement in Decision-Making. Performance-based measurement alters the contemporary roles of line officers and mid-management. Line officers will have to broaden their decision-making and problem-solving abilities and determine the best way to achieve desired results. Mid-managers will have to change the way they supervise employees -- instead of directing every move, they must serve as coaches and facilitators. These role changes may be threatening for those who are used to authoritarian and routinized operation. Proper training should be provided to facilitate these role changes and new responsibilities.

Flexible Management Style. A shift to performance-based measurement implies that an agency is open to the modification of practices and new ways of doing business. This requires a certain amount of risk-taking at the individual

Figure 22 - Process and Outcomes

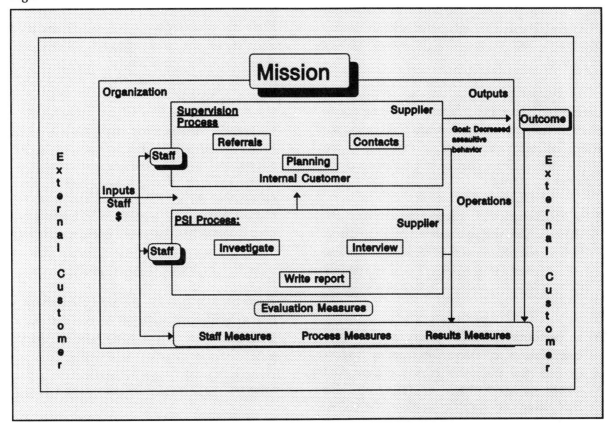

and organizational level. Managers must define appropriate operational boundaries while at the same time giving agency personnel the operational latitude and backing that risk-taking requires. Initial mistakes, or a failure to achieve desired results, should be met with a joint problem-solving approach among all levels of personnel, rather than discipline. A flexible management style encourages creativity and innovation and increases the likelihood of achieving the desired results.

Integrating Performance-Based Measurement with other Staff Duties. With more discretionary power comes more responsibility. Performance-based measurement differs from other forms of agency and program evaluation in that it is a system-wide, ongoing approach to mea-

suring and modifying agency opera-tions. Hence, staff at all levels of the organization must be involved in defining process and outcome measures, collecting and maintaining data, reviewing and reporting results, and modifying practices. Each officer should be responsible for collecting and maintaining data on their caseload; unit supervisors should be responsible for verifying caseload data through random audits, aggregating this caseload information, and compiling unit results; and so on up the ranks. Those responsible for collecting and maintaining data should be involved in developing procedures for collecting and reporting data. As with any new responsibility, agency staff should be thoroughly trained on all related procedures and evaluated accordingly. Performance-based measurement should not be viewed as a separate research or evaluation component with separate staffing requirements, but rather as a standard procedure that is fully integrated into all agency operations and the responsibility of all agency personnel.

A System of Internal Accountability. A system of checks and balances should be put in place to determine if appropriate procedures are being followed and to ensure that results are acted upon. These checks and balances could come in the form of:

- a designated staff member to oversee the development, implementation and modification of all policies and procedures related to performance-based measurement; to compile agency reports; and to disseminate information;

- a performance-based measurement team consisting of representatives from each agency unit and all levels of the organization whose members would be responsible for facilitating the proper implementation of performance-based measurement and all related procedures within their respective units; and

- a quality improvement team consisting of representatives from each agency unit and all levels of the organization whose members would be responsible for modifying programs and practices based on results, overseeing the implementation of improved practices within their units, and recognizing outstanding performance.

In all likelihood, to ensure agency-wide accountability for· performance-based measurement procedures and results, all three of these components will be needed. Broad involvement of this nature will promote commitment to procedures, results and improvements.

Technological Advances

Performance-based measurement systems require changes in the way agencies collect, enter, define and analyze data sets. In order to collect the most useful information in the most efficient way, it is recommended that any performance-based measurement strategy include a fully integrated management information system. Such a system would minimize the duplication of efforts and provide built-in expandability for future concerns. Please see *Appendix B, Recommendations for an Effective Management Information System*, for a guide to technical support for a system of performance-based measurement.

Putting It All Together

Agencies can use the following questions and tips to guide the selection of process and outcome measures. For each identified goal consider:

Who will be impacted by goal achievement?

- Think about performance measures as having internal and external consumers.

- Determine and prioritize what questions each group of consumers need to have answered.

- If an answer is not possible, be straightforward about the reasons.

- Process measures may be all that internal customers are interested in, while external customers will expect to see results as *they* define them.

- Remember that part of community corrections' responsibility to customers is to manage customers' expectations.

What is the most efficient method for obtaining credible information about goal achievement?

- Select methods that provide the best information possible within the constraints of time, experience and cost.

- Determine the time frame for getting answers to the questions.

- Do not let expedience rule -- paying lip service to the need for process and outcome evaluations wastes organizational resources and fools no one.

What human and financial resources are available or needed to obtain information about the extent of goal achievement?

- The support of all agency staff, particularly top management, is critical to planning a strategy for performance methods and even more important to carrying out that strategy.

- Getting and keeping staff support requires a frank discussion of expectations.

- The level of staff time allocated toward measuring agency/program results may, to a large extent, determine the process and outcome measures selected.

- A management information system facilitates the gathering, compilation and analysis of data, however, many questions can be answered through systematic, manual processes.

Careful consideration of these questions and points will help to guide agencies through the selection of process and outcome measures for assessing agency/program performance.

Conclusion

This model, for the development of a performance-based measurement strategy, will assist agencies in exploring important organizational issues. By clarifying their organizational values, mission, and goals agencies can more readily identify methods for measuring, evaluating, and communicating agency performance and accomplishments.

While the values and mission of the organization are relatively stable, they can and do change. Crisis, new leadership, new information, and first hand experiences can reinforce or shift existing values and missions. Such changes can contribute to organizational growth by forcing a reexamination of existing values and missions. The methods, or activities, used to support and achieve an agency's values and mission can be expected to change more frequently than the overall values or mission, particularly as more is learned about their effectiveness from the consistent measuring of results.

Resource constraints may influence the type and extent of system development. However, they should not dissuade agencies from developing a performance-based measurement system. Even the most rudimentary system for measuring results with performance-based measures is a step in the right direction. As agencies learn from employing basic measurement strategies, more advanced strategies can be introduced. If the commitment to performance-based measurement exists, an agency can apply the model outlined within this chapter. The next module demonstrates the model's utility within a hypothetical community corrections agency -- Anytown, USA.

MODULE II

A WORKING MODEL FOR PERFORMANCE-BASED MEASUREMENT

MODULE II

A WORKING MODEL FOR PERFORMANCE-BASED MEASUREMENT

Module Overview

This module is designed to put the model for developing performance-based measures into practice. Each chapter is devoted to a specific goal identified for a hypothetical agency, the Anytown, USA Community Corrections Department. The chapters include:

- *Chapter Three: Assist Decisionmakers*
- *Chapter Four: Enforce Court/Parole Board-Ordered Sanctions*
- *Chapter Five: Protect the Community*
- *Chapter Six: Assist Offenders to Change*
- *Chapter Seven: Support Crime Victims*
- *Chapter Eight: Coordinate and Promote Use of Community Services*

This module demonstrates methods for identifying agency-specific process and outcome measures. Each chapter discusses: the rationale for the goal; activities conducted to achieve the goal; and possible measures for determining if activities and services were delivered as planned and the extent of goal achievement. The outcomes listed are legitimate measures for each respective goal; they are not all inclusive lists and may not reflect measures appropriate for all agencies. Many of the identified process and outcome measures could be used to assess the success of several goals. For example, "a reduction in positive drug test results" could be used as a measure of success for three goals: enforcing court-ordered sanctions, protecting the community, and assisting offenders to change. In the interest of time and space, each outcome measure will only appear in one chapter. The values, mission, and goals appearing in Figures 23-25 will serve as the basis for the performance-based measurement strategy outlined within this module.

Figure 23 - Values Statement

Anytown, USA
Community Corrections Department

VALUES STATEMENT:

The Anytown, USA Community Corrections Department believes in its ability to protect the public through the effective provision of supervision and services that promote behavioral change in offenders and deter and/or prevent further criminal activity by offenders under their supervision.

The Anytown, USA Community Corrections Department will provide services to offenders in a fair and equitable manner without discrimination or disparity.

The Anytown, USA Community Corrections Department will operate its programs in a parsimonious manner to conserve agency resources and to provide the maximum amount of services to offenders and the community.

The Anytown, USA Community Corrections Department will be accountable to its stakeholders through effective financial management and the demonstration of positive program results.

The Anytown, USA Community Corrections Department supports the rights of victims by facilitating and enforcing the payment of restitution and other reparations to victims and/or the community.

The Anytown, USA Community Corrections Department will conduct investigations and provide information to the court and parole board in a timely and professional manner to assist in the decision-making process.

The Anytown, USA Community Corrections Department will uphold the orders of the court and parole board and maintain program credibility through the fair and consistent enforcement of supervisory conditions.

The Anytown, USA Community Corrections Department believes in offenders' ability to change and will provide activities and services designed to facilitate change and to help them become productive members of society.

Figure 24 - Mission Statement

Anytown, USA
Community Corrections Department

MISSION STATEMENT:

The mission of the Anytown, USA Community Corrections Department is to enhance the safety of victims and communities through the fair and effective supervision of community-based offenders, community partnerships, and results-driven management practices.

Figure 25 - Goal Statement

Anytown, USA
Community Corrections Department

GOAL STATEMENTS:

The Anytown, USA Community Corrections Department will:

1) provide information and recommendations to assist decisionmakers in determining the appropriate disposition of cases;

2) enforce all sanctions ordered by the courts and paroling authority;

3) protect the community through appropriate assessment, intervention, surveillance, and enforcement activities;

4) assist offenders to change through thorough assessment of needs and appropriate interventions;

5) support crime victims by remaining sensitive to their concerns and by addressing their needs and interests throughout the processing, supervision and termination of a case; and

6) coordinate and promote the use of community services to maximize available community resources and meet the needs of its offenders.

CHAPTER THREE

ASSIST DECISIONMAKERS

> **GOAL:**   The Anytown, USA Community Corrections Department will provide information and recommendations to assist decisionmakers in determining the appropriate disposition of cases.

Introduction

Throughout the criminal justice continuum, there are several impact points where decisionmakers (i.e., judges and parole boards) must determine the appropriate dispositions for offenders. In most cases, these decisionmakers are given discretion, or latitude, in the decisionmaking process. By providing these decisionmakers with information and recommendations, probation and parole agencies and officers play an important role in guiding that discretion.

During the sentencing, release, and revocation process it is essential that decisionmakers have complete and accurate information regarding offenders' backgrounds and their current risks and needs. Judges and parole boards often depend on the investigative and analytical skills of probation and parole officers for gathering and reporting this information and for recommending appropriate dispositions. The focus of this chapter will be on discussing the importance of this role to the decisionmaking process, the activities conducted by probation and parole agencies to assist decisionmakers, and process and outcome measures for evaluating how effectively agencies fulfill this function.

Rationale for Goal

As illustrated in Figure 26, there are several key impact points in the sentencing and supervision processes where decisions must be made regarding an offender's behavior. Probation and parole agencies provide parallel services to the court and parole board, respectively, at each of these impact points by providing information and recommendations to guide discretion and assist with decisions regarding case dispositions.

In *Offender Assessment and Evaluation: The Presentence Investigation Report* (Clear, Clear & Burrell, 1989), the authors cite three key reasons why discretion will remain an important element of judicial decisions:

1) Goal ambiguity - the goals of sentencing include retribution, deterrence, incapacitation and rehabilitation. These goals are often conflicting. "In some cases, aspects of the criminal act may call for a heavily punitive sanction, while in other cases the special circumstances of the offender will call for leniency in support of rehabilitation" (p. 12).

2) Human differences - personal factors including an offender's age, attitude, criminal history and living situation will influence sentencing decisions.

Figure 26 - Decision Points

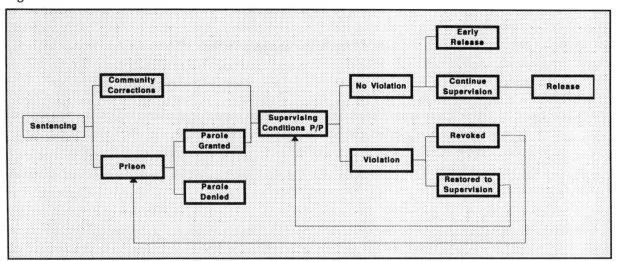

3) Uncertainty - the "correctness" of judicial decisions is dependent on sometimes unpredictable human behavior. Regardless of how sophisticated risk assessment processes become, there will always be an element of uncertainty.

Discretion is also a factor for other decision points appearing in the flow chart. It is this discretion and the above mentioned reasons for its continuing existence that provide the basis for this critical goal within probation and parole.

Judges in courts across the United States have a number of sources for advice on the disposition of each case. It is their role to listen to the advice from each of these sources and to arrive at a fair disposition of the case. In many situations, the information sources have a vested interest in the case. The prosecutor may need to maintain a "tough" stance on criminal activity. The defense is paid to "represent the best interests" of the defendant. The crime victim(s) suffered as a result of the criminal act and want to see the defendant "justly" punished. Family and friends of the defendant believe a mistake was made and mercy should be shown.

The judge must weigh information from each of these sources in the process of arriving at an unbiased decision regarding the defendant's case. "The major problem facing judges is the uncertainty involved in all sentencing decisions, except the most extreme cases. Anything that helps to reduce the uncertainty of a decision is considered information" (Clear et al., 1989, p. 14). One source of reliable information is presentence investigation reports (PSIs).

Most states require, by statute, that a presentence investigation be conducted, and a report prepared, to assist judges in the sentencing of felony defendants. The American Bar Association (1970) stated that "the primary purpose of the presentence report is to provide the sentencing court with succinct and precise information upon which to base a rational sentencing decision" (p. 11). The PSI becomes an important document and is used for purposes beyond initial sentencing including:

• serving as the basis for a plan of probation or parole supervision and treatment;

- assisting jail and prison personnel in their classification and treatment programs;

- furnishing parole authorities with information pertinent to consideration for parole and release planning; and

- providing a source of information for research in criminal justice (Abadinsky, 1991).

Responsibility for the presentence investigation generally falls within the purview of probation departments. While the content and depth of presentence reports varies across jurisdictions, they typically include information on the seriousness of the crime, the defendant's risk, the defendant's circumstances, and a summary of the sentencing options (Clear et al., 1989). The PSI generally concludes with a recommendation for the disposition of the case based on statutory guidelines. Follow-up recidivism studies have shown that probation officers are effective in determining which defendants are suitable for probation (Langan & Cunniff, 1992).

When an offender is being considered for parole, a similar process to that used in judicial sentencing is implemented. Institutional parole officers prepare a case file for the parole board that generally includes the PSI, institutional reports regarding treatment and misconduct, and a release plan in the event that parole is granted (Abadinsky, 1991).

Sentencing and release decisions are only two examples of when probation or parole officers are asked to provide information and recommendations. Violations of probation or parole conditions require action and/or recommendations by the officers involved. Agency policies and procedures and the severity of the violation will determine if the recommendation is made to a probation or parole administrator or if the offender is to be brought before the court or parole board. Information regarding the nature of the violation and the offender's general performance on probation and parole is provided to the sentencing judge or a hearing officer representing the parole board. A recommendation is made regarding continuance on probation/parole, sanctions to be imposed, or revocation. This recommendation is generally based on the offender's overall performance on probation/parole, current attitudes toward the violation, and the level of risk the violating behavior creates.

Probation and parole officers will also make recommendations for changes in the level of offenders' supervision within the department. The recommendation will be based upon changes in the offender's situation that warrant an increased or decreased level of supervision. Recommendations are also made for early termination from supervision for those offenders successfully completing supervisory conditions.

Probation/parole officers are the eyes and ears of the court/parole board. When reporting information and offering recommendations, probation and parole officers should remain objective and unbiased. Sentencing, release, and revocation decisions determine the level of freedom accorded an offender and the extent of public protection. These two very important outcomes make it imperative that information provided to courts and parole boards is timely, accurate and complete.

A key concern of probation and parole officers and agencies is that decisions made by the judiciary and parole board often constrain agency operations. Probation and parole personnel have suggested that judicial and parole board decisions frequently result in the inappropriate placement of offenders, be it traditional supervision, intensive supervision or prison. Another common lament is that judicial and parole board philosophies or policies are sometimes too stringent or too lenient regarding violations of, and responses to, supervisory conditions. Policies that are too stringent make it impossible to work effectively with offenders on long term goals involving behavioral change, while policies that are too lenient make it difficult to hold offenders accountable and enforce court- or parole board-ordered sanctions. Considering such impacts of decisionmakers, assisting them becomes an important goal for probation and parole agencies.

Probation and Parole Activities

Conduct Investigations

Probation and parole agencies are responsible for conducting investigations to verify information obtained from offenders. Investigations are generally conducted at the presentence and pre-release stages and in response to a violation of probation/parole.

The following information is typically gathered for the presentence investigation:

- criminal history - prior offenses and dispositions;

- details of the current offense - information from the arrest report, a statement from the defendant, and a statement from the victim of the offense;

- social history - family relationships, marital status, dependents, interests and activities, residence history and religious affiliations;

- military record;

- medical history and psychological summary;

- educational background, present employment status, financial status, and capabilities;

- home and neighborhood environment; and

- reports from clinics, institutions, and other social agencies with which the defendant has been involved (APPA, 1991).

The following areas are typically investigated for parole hearings:

- the appropriateness of the offender's proposed residency;

- opportunities for employment upon release;

- adjustment to prison - behavior, participation in rehabilitative or educational programming, and work assignments; and

- victim input regarding the offender's release (Abadinsky, 1991).

One means of gathering this information is to have the defendant complete a detailed questionnaire providing the bulk of the above information. The investigator then pursues further information through a variety of methods, including mailed requests for information, telephone calls and interviews. Information is obtained from schools the defendant has attended, previous and current employers, community service providers with whom the defendant has been involved, and other collateral sources. The defendant's family is often a good source of information, and home visits are sometimes conducted during investigations to observe the defendant's home and neighborhood environment. The law enforcement agency involved in a defendant's arrest is contacted for their perspective regarding the defendant's involvement in the offense, level of cooperation, and perceived attitude toward authority. A key source of information during the presentence/pre-release investigations are victims of the offenses.

Probation/parole officers are often responsible for soliciting victim input on the defendant's sentencing or release from prison and for gathering information regarding mental, emotional or physical harm, and any loss or damage to property created by the offense.

Violation investigations are typically a bit less extensive. The officer may discuss the violating behavior with family members to get a sense of whether or not this behavior is part of an overall pattern of noncompliance or an aberration. School personnel, employers, community service providers, and law enforcement agencies are often contacted to ascertain the defendant's performance in other areas.

The purpose of these investigations is to gain input from individuals with varying perspectives on the defendant's behavior. Clear et al., (1989) offer three common tests to determine when enough information has been gathered: 1) when the investigator is 90 percent confident that the best decision is known; 2) when a pattern begins to emerge in the facts learned; and 3) when the continued investigation turns up redundant information. Often patterns emerge that suggest whether or not the defendant is likely to comply with supervisory conditions and the level of risk the defendant poses to the community. A comprehensive, well-balanced investigation is critical to the PSI and, ultimately, the decisionmaking process.

Assess Offender Risks and Needs

Probation and parole agencies may assess the risks and needs of offenders as part of the above mentioned investigations. This appraisal assists the judge/parole board in determining the level of risk the offender poses to the community and to him- or herself, and identifies areas of need that contribute to the criminal behavior. A standard process is generally utilized to determine the severity of an offender's problems,

evaluate contributing factors, and appraise personal and social resources. This process may include one or both of the following methods:

- actuarial assessments - this is perhaps the most common method for assessing risks and needs within the criminal justice system. It involves the use of quantifiable, standardized, objective instruments designed to measure static and dynamic factors predictive of criminal behavior; and

- clinical assessments - these assessments are subjective evaluations of the offender based on professional judgement or intuition.

These offender assessments can be conducted by a probation/parole officer or by an outside service provider to whom the offender is referred. Assessment protocol may also include a more detailed evaluation of specific problem areas such as drug/alcohol abuse, sexual deviance, or mental health.

Assessments may be conducted at several key impact points. Some agencies conduct risk/need assessments at the presentence/pre-release stage and include them in the PSI or parole plan to assist courts/parole boards in sentencing/release decisions, establishing supervisory conditions, and/or in determining the appropriate program placement (e.g., half-way house, electronic monitoring, intensive supervision, regular supervision). Many agencies conduct reassessments on a periodic basis, typically every six months, upon which changes in the level or type of supervision are based. Although less frequently, risk/need assessments are sometimes conducted when a violation occurs to help determine the level of risk an offender poses to the community and to assist with sanctioning decisions.

The risk/need assessments conducted for these purposes may or may not be the same assessments used in the supervisory process to classify offenders and allocate resources. Some agencies have excluded the use of risk classification instruments from these decisionmaking processes to avoid legal challenges regarding the validity of the instrument, asserting that the instruments were designed for classification and other supervisory purposes rather than to assist decisionmakers in determining case dispositions. Risk/need assessment will be more fully explored in Chapters 5 and 6 of the monograph.

Compile and Document Information

An abundance of information is gathered throughout the investigative activities outlined above. The next task for probation and parole officers is to compile the information into a manageable format for decisionmakers. It is imperative for decisionmakers to be able to quickly get a complete and accurate picture of the defendant's criminal or violating behaviors. This is largely dependent on an officer's writing and reporting skills. It is also dependent on an officer's ability to report facts versus opinions and to remain objective when compiling the information. "The PSI[R] serves the critical role of quality control on the system's ordinary processes, making certain that decisions are not irrational, and that important factors have not been overlooked" (Clear et al., 1989, p. 22). Documentation is very important during the investigation and decisionmaking stages. Documented facts about the defendant's background will guide judicial/parole board discretion in a fair and equitable manner. The following pages contain a sample PSI.

This is just one example of a PSI. The format, length, and content of PSI's vary across the nation. The information contained in PSIs is critical as it is used as the basis for subsequent decisions regarding offenders' dispositions.

Recommend a Sentence, Disposition, and/or Administrative Decision

The final task involved in assisting decisionmakers is to make recommendations for the appropriate disposition of a case. Probation/parole officers make recommendations regarding the:

- initial sentencing of a case;
- release from prison/jail (i.e., shock probation);
- release on parole;
- supervisory conditions of probation/parole; and
- responses to violations of supervisory conditions.

Recommendations for sentencing and for release on parole are typically guided by statutes on considerations for probation or parole. Officers are responsible for analyzing the available information on the defendant, considering the statute and making recommendations. There is research to substantiate the effectiveness of probation officers' role in this process. In a study of 306,000 felons sentenced to probation in 1986, Langan & Cunniff (1992) found defendants who were not recommended for probation were nearly twice as likely to have their sentence revoked and sent to prison (37%) as those recommended for probation (22%).

Recommendations for specific supervisory conditions of a defendant can be made based upon findings from investigations and assessments of risk and need. Every effort should be made in the recommendation to match services with offender needs. Including special conditions, such as drug/alcohol treatment, as a part of a probation sentence provides the legal leverage that many offenders require to begin addressing needs related to their criminal behavior. Figure 28 includes the recommendation for the sentencing of Robert Davis.

Figure 27 - Presentence Investigation Report: Robert J. Davis

---

PRESENTENCE INVESTIGATION REPORT

Name: Robert J. Davis (W/M) Age: 22   DOB: 4/14/70

Address: 325 W. Maple Avenue, Springfield 50532

Information for this report was obtained from the following sources:

Official Police Report
Criminal records check
Educational records
Employment records
Report from the Mental Health Department
Health records from the Health Department and the Hospital Emergency Room

Interviews were conducted with:

Robert J. Davis
Mrs. Raymond Davis, his mother
Mrs. Diane Davis, his wife
Mr. Doug Franklin, High School Principal

<u>Current Charge</u>

The defendant is charged with Domestic Violence, a felony of the fourth degree. The official police report indicates that on September 15, 1993 an emergency call was received from Mrs. Diane Davis who indicated that her husband, Robert Davis, had just "beat her up and threatened to take her child." Mrs. Davis further indicated that her husband was very drunk. By the time Police Officer Conlin arrived at the home, Robert was gone. Officer Conlin interviewed Mrs. Davis who indicated that she and her husband had been fighting over Robert coming home drunk, that he punched her in the mouth and around the head several times and pushed her to the floor. Mrs. Davis was bleeding and said she had a headache. She was taken to the emergency room for treatment. There were no witnesses to this event, although several neighbors indicated that they had witnessed Robert hitting Mrs. Davis on several previous occasions. Robert was arrested at his mother's home, 325 W. Maple Avenue, the following day.

<u>Criminal History</u>

According to Mrs. Davis and Robert, he had several encounters with the juvenile justice system before turning 18. While he was in foster care, he ran away several times. These incidents were treated as status offenses, and he was placed in different foster homes each time.

When he moved to Springfield, there were reports to juvenile court for repeated truancy problems. Robert was arrested as a juvenile for possession of a controlled substance on school grounds and for shoplifting. There was also a charge resulting from the physical assault of a classmate. Robert claims this occurred when the other student became too friendly with his (Robert's) girlfriend, and he (Robert) had to "teach him a lesson."

The following charges have been filed since Robert became an adult:

Date: August 15, 1988
Charge: Shoplifting
Disposition: The store agreed to drop the charges so Mr. Davis could attend an educational program which he stated he planned to enter in September.

Date: March 23, 1989
Charge: Drunk and Disorderly
Disposition: Several persons were arrested during a loud party at 1629 North 28th Street. However, the charges were dismissed.

Date: July 3, 1990
Charge: Possession of Marijuana
Disposition: Mr. Davis was arrested for being in possession of 6 ounces of marijuana. He was diverted from adjudication by agreeing to attend a drug treatment program.

Date: April 20, 1991
Charge: Trafficking a Controlled Substance
Disposition: Mr. Davis was arrested for trying to sell marijuana to a minor. However, the charges were dropped when the minor refused to testify.

Date: October 8, 1991
Charge: Assault
Disposition: Police were called to the scene of a domestic dispute at a duplex on W. Oak Street. Mr. Davis was arrested for assaulting his wife. However, she later refused to press charges, and he was released.

There is currently an emergency protective order in force prohibiting Mr. Davis from coming within 1,000 feet of his wife, Diane Davis or daughter, Debbie.

Family and Background Information

Robert Jefferson Davis (W/M) was born 4/14/70 in Midvale in Washington County. He is the second of six children born to Raymond and Minnie Davis. Raymond Davis was a truck driver and farmer. Mrs. Davis was a homemaker.

Mrs. Davis said her husband had a drinking problem and had difficulty keeping employment and supporting his family. She reported that when her husband drank, he was often abusive to her and the children. They had frequent separations during their marriage, and at these times she received AFDC benefits. She said there was never enough money to meet all the needs of the family, and they lived in substandard housing without running water for several years. Mr. Davis was killed in a vehicle crash in 1982 when Robert was 12 years old. Mr. Davis was intoxicated at the time of the crash which also killed his passenger and permanently disabled another driver.

Mrs. Davis said that she completed the eighth grade and her husband, Raymond, completed the sixth grade. Mrs. Davis did not work until the family moved to Springfield in 1984. Since then she has worked as a cook in a diner on Third Street. The family lives at 325 W. Maple in a rented home that is in very bad repair. Robert's older sister, Ramona, and younger sister, Rebecca, have both married and left home. However, Mrs. Davis reports that Rebecca's marriage is shaky and she has repeatedly returned home with her two small children for several weeks at a time. Three younger brothers still live at home: Richard, 18 is a 10th grade drop out and is unemployed; Roy, 16 is still enrolled but seldom attends school; and Roger, 14 attends special education classes at Valley Middle School.

Mrs. Davis reports that in 1983-84 her children were removed from her care and placed in foster care. She moved to Springfield in 1984 and asked that her children be returned. She said that here in the city, the "welfare people" and neighbors are not as "nosey" and she doesn't have to worry about losing her kids.

Mrs. Davis reported that Robert's birth and early development were normal. She said he was always an active child and had to be watched carefully. She said she spanked him often as a young child but it never seemed to do much good.

Education

Robert Davis attended Midvale Elementary School from 1976 - 1983. He attended Simpson Elementary School and Johnson Middle School in 1983-84 while in foster care. In 1984 he enrolled in Eastside Middle School in Springfield, and in 1985 he entered East Washington County High School. His attendance in elementary school and while living in foster care was good. However, upon moving to Springfield, his school attendance became very poor, and he dropped out of school in 1985 at the end of the ninth grade.

Robert Davis' school records show poor and failing grades beginning with fourth grade. Psychological tests administered by the school indicated that Robert had some learning disabilities and he was placed in resource classes for special help with reading. His math abilities were low average. During the ninth grade at East Washington County High School, Robert received several disciplinary reports and suspensions and was placed in a Behavior Disorder special classroom for the last half of the year. At the time he quit school Robert's test scores showed that he was reading on a fourth grade level and his math skills were at sixth grade level. The High School Principal, Doug Franklin, commented that Robert could be a very likeable youth, but was poorly motivated to do well in school. He said that Robert seemed to gravitate toward the wrong crowd and was easily led into trouble by his peers. He said Robert tended to act without thinking about the consequences. He was also easily angered if peers teased him. He had several verbal confrontations with teachers and a few fights with other students.

Mr. Franklin said Robert became jealous easily and several girlfriends had "set him up" to get in fights with other guys.

Employment

The following employment has been verified for Robert Davis:

1985-86   Jones' Car Wash, 1576 South Fourth Street. $3.35 per hour. Reason for leaving: failed to show up for work two weeks in a row. The owner of the business reported that initially Robert worked hard and was well-liked by other employees. However, as time passed, he became less dependable and tended to be careless about his work. When he confronted Robert, his attitude was usually sullen, but occasionally he became argumentative. He and other employees said they were glad when Robert finally just quit coming to work.

1986-88   Lawn mowing service, 712 S. First Street. $5.00 per lawn. Reason for leaving: the work was seasonal and Robert found another job in 1988. The owner of the business has left town and no additional information could be obtained.

1988-90   Truck and Freight Warehouse, Highway 48. $4.50 per hour. Reason for leaving: fired for stealing merchandise. The supervisor said Robert was a good employee when he was motivated, but he also could be lazy and sloppy in his work at times. The supervisor said he suspected Robert was drinking on the job but was never able to prove it. He said Robert had gotten into a serious fight with another employee one time and had injured the other man.

1990-92   Robert has worked at various construction jobs earning from $5.00 to $6.00 per hour as a general laborer. This work has been seasonal, and often he was hired as a day laborer. One foreman who supervised Robert on a job lasting several months spoke of his aptitude for carpentry work. However, again, he mentioned that he suspected a drinking problem, there were conflicts between Robert and other employees, and at times his attendance was poor.

Health and Mental Health

According to Mrs. Davis, Robert had the usual childhood illnesses, but was generally a healthy child. She said he had frequent colds during the winters because they did not have adequate heat in the house. However, she said he seldom missed school because of illness. He did not have any hospitalizations during his childhood.

The attending physician when Robert Davis was treated for a cut on his head sustained in the car crash before his arrest reported that he was in satisfactory general health but appeared slightly underweight for his height. He noted possible symptoms of vitamin deficiency, perhaps related to alcohol abuse. Robert is also nearsighted, and the doctor recommended a vision check-up.

Records from the Mental Health Center indicated that Robert Davis was evaluated for substance abuse in 1990 in lieu of prosecution on charges of possession of marijuana. The evaluation showed Robert did exhibit symptoms of alcoholism and reported the use of other drugs when he could get them. His mental health evaluation suggested he was immature and impulsive. He was assigned to an outpatient treatment program for substance abuse. His attendance was poor and he finally was dropped from the program. A letter was sent to the court reporting his discharge from the program.

Current Status

Robert Davis married Diane Smith in June 1989 after she became pregnant with their daughter. Robert said he married her so her parents would not press charges of statutory rape, as Diane was only 15. The couple lived with Diane's parents throughout their marriage, and Diane and their daughter, Debbie, still live with her parents.

Robert claims he has not really abused his wife; he only wanted to show her who was the "boss" in the family. However, Diane claims that he frequently hit her, and on two occasions she sought treatment in the emergency room for cuts and bruises he inflicted on her.

Robert and Diane have had frequent separations during their marriage. During these times, Robert always returned to his mother's home. Robert and Diane have been separated since the last violence occurred six months ago. There is a restraining order prohibiting Robert from coming within 1,000 feet of his wife or daughter.

Diane Davis said she would like to divorce Robert but does not have the money right now. She is working on her GED and hopes to attend a vocational training program next fall. Diane wants to take care of her daughter and get to the point that she can live independently from her parents. She does not envision that she and Robert will ever be able to live together again. Their daughter, Debbie, is 2 1/2 years old and appears to be developing normally for her age. Although he is ordered to do so, Robert does not currently pay any child support for his daughter.

Robert has been living with his mother for the past six months. She reports he does not contribute financially to the household, nor does he help out very often with cleaning, yard work or other chores around the house. She says he drinks too much just like his father did. She says she doesn't know where he gets the money to buy alcohol, but she suspects he has stolen money from her purse on occasions. Mrs. Davis seems a little overwhelmed with her responsibilities as a mother. She says she makes only $4.50 per hour working in the diner. She says her younger sons are following in Robert's footsteps and they are getting into trouble. She said she has had to miss work frequently to go to juvenile court with her younger sons.

Mrs. Davis appears to love her children, but does not have many skills for setting limits for them.

Robert says he "hangs out" with the two young men who were with him the night of his arrest and a few other "buddies" that he gets along with. A check indicated that all those he mentioned have criminal histories similar to his.

Robert says he would like to work as a carpenter in the future. He says he enjoyed the construction jobs he had and would like to learn more skills so he could make better wages. He said he enjoys woodworking and would someday like to have a small furniture-building shop of his own.

Figure 28 - Recommendation for Robert Davis

It is respectfully recommended that Robert Davis be placed on probation. This is the defendant's first felony conviction. He has been charged several times with both misdemeanor and felony offenses although in each case the charges were dropped. Robert's criminal record suggests that all previous charges and the instant conviction were drug or alcohol related. Robert's mother, wife and previous employer all stated that they believed Robert had an alcohol problem. A mental health report also indicated that Robert showed symptoms of alcoholism. The nature of the previous offense and statements from Robert's wife suggest that he is physically abusive when under the influence of alcohol. Robert was involved with the juvenile probation department but has not been under probation supervision since he became an adult. Robert could benefit from the structure and requirements of probation. It is recommended that, as a special condition of probation, Robert be required to undergo a comprehensive assessment at the Mental Health Center regarding his drug/alcohol abuse and domestic violence and that he be required to follow through with any treatment recommended. It is also recommended that Robert be prohibited from contacting his wife or daughter until further order of the court.

Probation or parole officers recommend actions for offenders who violate the conditions of their supervision. Depending upon departmental policies and the severity of the violation, the recommendation may be presented to the court/parole board or to a supervisor within the agency. When making the recommendation, the officer will consider the nature of the violation, the offender's overall performance on probation/parole, and the level of risk that the offender poses to the community. Over the last decade, a range of intermediate sanctions have been developed to respond to violations such as increased supervisory contacts, community service hours, or house arrest. The objective is to impose the least restrictive sanction likely to produce the desired behavior and hold the offender accountable. Revocation and reincarceration are, more and more, seen as a last resort.

Performance-Based Measures

The previous section outlined some of the probation or parole activities associated with assisting decisionmakers in determining the appropriate dispositions. The next step in the process is to identify performance-based measures that can be used to determine the degree to which probation or parole successfully fulfill this function. Process measures are required to determine if the agency is actually delivering the services and products designed to assist decisionmakers; outcome measures are needed to determine the results of these services and products. Examples of both are provided.

Process Measures

Percent of PSIs Completed on Time. The percent of PSIs completed on time reflects on the workload and resources of the officers and the agency. If a high percentage of reports are not being completed on time, possible reasons should be explored. One possible explanation is that the workload exceeds the capacity of the investigative staff. Another possible explanation is that some, or all, of the officers are not carrying their weight. In either situation, the information can be used to improve agency performance. If workload issues are apparent, the information can be used to justify requests for additional personnel. If the problem is officer efficiency, the information can be used to evaluate personnel, identify problem areas, and recommend actions to correct the problem(s).

Figure 29 - Percent of PSI's Completed on Time

Objective: 95% of all PSIs requested in the Anytown, USA Community Corrections Dept. will be completed on time.

Data elements: Number of PSIs completed on time, number of PSIs requested.

Formula: (Number of PSIs completed on time ÷ number of PSIs requested) x 100.

Example: 585 PSIs were requested during the first quarter of 1994. 562 were completed and returned on time.

(562 ÷ 585) x 100 = 96% of PSIs were completed on time. **Objective was achieved.**

Degree of Accuracy and Completeness of PSIs. Accurate and complete information is essential for judges and administrators to make sound decisions, and for establishing the credibility of the agency and its presentence investigation officers. To determine the degree of accuracy and completeness of PSIs, an agency could develop a procedure for randomly selecting and reviewing PSIs. For example, during each quarter, the supervisor could randomly

select ten PSIs prepared by each officer. The reports could be rated on accuracy and completeness based on predetermined criteria such as:

Figure 30 - Degree of Accuracy and Completeness of PSIs

Objective: 90% of all PSIs in the Anytown, USA Community Corrections Department will be complete and accurate when they are submitted to the court.

Data elements: Number of PSIs evaluated by supervisors, number of PSIs rated complete and accurate by supervisors.

Formula: (Number PSIs rated complete and accurate by supervisors ÷ number of PSIs evaluated) x 100.

Example: 60 of the 585 PSIs completed in the first quarter of 1994 were randomly selected for review (10%). 51 of the PSIs met minimum standards for accuracy and completeness.

(51 ÷ 60) x 100 = 85% of all PSIs were rated complete and accurate. **Objective was not achieved.**

- Grammatical and spelling errors - Poorly written reports are likely to bring the value of the PSI into low esteem with judges. This could be detrimental to the defendant and/or society if the recommendations are discounted, even in part, by such considerations.

- Thoroughness of case analysis - Have all relevant goals in the disposition of the case been considered (e.g., reparation, crime prevention, retribution)? Has the impact of the victim been thoroughly and accurately assessed?

- Parsimony - Has the PSI officer considered all less intrusive options consistent with the goals of sentencing?

- Cost consciousness - Has the PSI officer considered all less expensive options consistent with the goals of sentencing?

- Equity/disparity - Is the PSI officer consistently more or less lenient/harsh than other PSI officers in recommending sanctions to decisionmakers?

The extent to which agencies can reduce unwarranted disparity in investigations and recommendations of different officers (e.g., through training and supervision/monitoring of criteria such as those outlined above) is a very important measure of the extent to which the agency is doing its job in an equitable and just way.

Outcome Measures

Percent of Offenders Receiving the Recommended Sentence. A number of factors affect the final decisions of a case including the philosophy of the judge/parole board, plea bargains, and sentencing alternatives. A recommendation based upon complete and accurate information and sound professional judgement is more likely to be accepted.

Documenting the percent of recommendations accepted and the decisionmaker's rationale for deviating from the recommendation may provide insight regarding their philosophies and the type of information helpful to decisionmakers. It may also provide an opportunity to educate the judiciary/parole board on the effectiveness of various programs, or components, with specific types of offenders.

Percent of Offenders Recommended for and Successfully Completing Probation/Parole Supervision. A final means of evaluating PSIs and

Figure 31 - Percent of Offenders Receiving Recommended Sentence

Objective: 75% of all offenders in the Anytown, USA Community Corrections Department will receive the sentence recommended as a result of the PSI investigation.

Data Elements: Number of PSI investigations, number of offenders who received the recommended sentence.

Formula: (Number of offenders who received the recommended sentence ÷ number of PSI investigations completed) x 100.

Example: 585 PSI investigations were completed during the first quarter of 1994. 462 offenders received the sentence recommended in the PSI report.

(462 ÷ 585) x 100 = 79% of the PSI recommendations for were accepted. **Objective was achieved.**

recommendations is to determine the supervision outcome of offenders recommended for probation/parole (i.e., what percent of offenders recommended for community supervision successfully completed their term of probation/parole). This information can serve as *one* indicator of officers' investigation and assessment skills. A high rate of success for those offenders recommended for community supervision would reinforce an agency's ability to identify appropriate offenders for community supervision.

If an agency decides to use this outcome measure, extreme care must always be taken to evaluate the outside influences and variables that contribute to case outcomes. Being held accountable for this outcome creates a danger that officers may become more conservative and

Figure 32 - Percent of Offenders Recommended for and Successfully Completing Probation/Parole Supervision

Objective: 70% of all offenders recommended for, and placed on, community supervision in the Anytown, USA Community Corrections Department will successfully complete the required period of supervision.

Data Elements: Number of offenders recommended for community supervision, number of offenders successfully completing supervision.

Formula: (Number of offenders successfully completing supervision ÷ number of offenders recommended for community supervision) * 100

Example: 430 offenders were recommended for, and placed on, community supervision during the first quarter of 1990. Of those 430 offenders, 318 successfully completed their terms of supervision.

(318 ÷ 430) * 100 = 74% of all offenders recommended for community supervision during 1994 successfully completed their supervision requirements. **Objective was achieved.**

Judges and parole boards are dependant on the investigative and analytical skills of officers for making informed case decisions. It is imperative that community corrections agencies and officers be provided with training and resources which allow for the high quality performance of this function. The extent to which agencies are successful at providing comprehensive, accurate and timely information to decisionmakers directly impacts the professional relationships established between community corrections and the judiciary/parole board. Furthermore, it affects other agency goals by impacting the number and type of offenders placed on probation/parole, supervisory conditions imposed upon offenders, and the enforcement of those conditions. Performance-based measures, such as those discussed above, will assist administrators in modifying and improving agency practices to ensure the achievement of this crucial goal. The far reaching consequences of the activities conducted to assist decisionmakers will be further revealed throughout the next goal-specific chapters.

risk-aversive in their recommendations to the court/parole board. A better measure might be the degree of fit between the precise services and controls recommended and those actually achieved (e.g., percentage completing educational requirements; percentage fulfilling court-ordered financial obligations).

Conclusion

As can be seen, assisting decisionmakers is a critical goal for probation and parole agencies.

CHAPTER FOUR

ENFORCE COURT/PAROLE BOARD-ORDERED SANCTIONS

> **GOAL:** The Anytown, USA Community Corrections Department will enforce all sanctions ordered by the courts and paroling authorities.

Introduction

The emergence of intermediate sanction programs over the past decade has resulted in increased responsibilities for community corrections agencies. More offenders with higher levels of risk are being placed under some type of community supervision, often with more stringent conditions and increased court/parole board-ordered obligations. Probation and parole officers are charged with the enforcement of these supervisory conditions. The extent to which agencies are successful in accomplishing the previously discussed goal of "assisting decisionmakers" may impact the number, type and reasonableness of conditions needing enforced. Nevertheless, enforcing court/parole board-ordered conditions is an important and difficult responsibility. It requires facilitation skills, ongoing monitoring and timely responses to progress and noncompliance. This chapter outlines the underlying rationale of supervisory conditions, basic activities related to their enforcement, and performance-based measures for assessing goal achievement.

Rationale for Goal

Historically, the criminal justice system has relied on the polar extremes of routine probation or traditional forms of incarceration.

Fears about inadequate control and punishment of high-risk probationers on the one hand and concern about the ineffectiveness, unconstitutional crowding, and soaring construction and maintenance costs of penal institutions on the other have prompted widespread calls for more extensive development and use of midrange, intermediate sanctions (Harland, 1993, p. 35).

Numerous new programs have been developed to meet the challenge of providing a level of punishment between traditional probation supervision and incarceration. Boot camps, diversion centers, electronic monitoring, intensive probation supervision, and house arrest serve as examples of the new breed of community corrections programs.

Intermediate sanctions have been given a wide and varied mission. Policymakers hope that by creating a new array of sanctioning programs they will make sentencing more just and effective for offenders, enhance public safety, increase local corrections capacity, contain growth in prison and jail populations, and reduce costs (McGarry, 1993, p. 11).

Inherent in the development of these sanctions, and the increasing number and type of offenders being sentenced to them, is an increase in the type of court orders imposed. Today a community supervision sentence may include drug testing, curfews, house arrest, electronic monitoring, court ordered treatment, community service, and/or restitution.

Such supervisory conditions of probation and parole are designed to:

• punish offenders;

• hold them accountable for their crime;

• constrain or incapacitate;

• rehabilitate; and

• reduce an offender's risk to society.

Typically, all offenders on probation/parole within a jurisdiction are subject to several standard conditions (e.g., you shall report to your officer as directed; you shall not violate any laws). The number of core conditions varies from agency to agency. Often, special conditions are imposed by the court/parole board depending on the individual risks and needs of an offender. These conditions are generally of a rehabilitative nature (e.g., drug/alcohol treatment, job training) or more incapacitative (e.g., electronic monitoring, house arrest).

Violations of court/parole board-ordered conditions are generally referred to as *technical violations* (Abadinsky, 1991). Technical violations have long been thought of as an indication that the offender is 'going bad' and returning to criminal behavior (Petersilia & Turner, 1990). It is argued that public safety can be achieved by responding to these violations (i.e., through revocation and incarceration) and 'pre-empting' further criminal activity (Nidorf, 1991; Wagner, 1989). While there is some evidence that challenges this hypothesis (Greene, 1988; Petersilia & Turner, 1993) it is a key consideration in the

enforcement of court/parole board-ordered conditions.

Enforcing court and parole board orders is a primary function of probation and parole officers. Officers must facilitate compliance with court/parole board orders through intervention and supervision strategies aimed at ensuring that the offender has the capability and resources to comply; monitor offender compliance through various surveillance techniques; and enforce conditions by responding to non-compliance. With the advent of additional intermediate sanctions, as well as new technologies such as electronic monitoring equipment and drug testing, agency administrators can expect increased responsibilities for probation and parole officers.

Probation and Parole Activities

Facilitate Compliance

Probation and parole officers are responsible for explaining the supervisory conditions to offenders. The offender's signature is generally required to represent the fact that the conditions are understood and accepted. Many conditions are straightforward -- the offender either complies or not. Examples may include:

• you will not leave the county without prior permission of your probation officer; and

• you will not own, purchase or possess any firearms.

Other conditions, while seemingly straightforward, may require the assistance of the probation/parole officer. For example, most agencies have a condition requiring employment. To facilitate compliance with this condition, an officer must first determine what factors contribute to an offender's unemployment (e.g., laziness, lack of skills, lack of transportation, child care constraints). These identified factors will drive the development of a supervision strategy and may ultimately impact monitoring and enforcement techniques. Table 4 depicts how the factors contributing to an offender's unemployment result in very different supervision strategies.

Both supervision strategies are aimed at facilitating compliance with the supervisory condition of employment. Sam's supervision strategy is focused more on the rehabilitative goal of sentencing by teaching and modeling job seeking and employment skills. Robert's supervision strategy, while also concerned with rehabilitation, is focused more on promoting accountability by requiring specific steps toward obtaining and maintaining employment or schooling. Both strategies provide structure and, in that sense, serve an incapacitative function.

Robert's supervision strategy addresses his apparent needs while also holding him accountable for the court-ordered condition of obtaining employment. Requiring Robert to perform community service or "work for free" accomplishes several objectives: 1) it minimizes his leisure time; 2) it provides motivation to obtain a paying job; and 3) it teaches him responsibility and possible job skills.

Merely stating a condition and expecting compliance sets the probation/parole agency and the offender up for failure. It is their refusal or inability to follow rules, due to factors such as antisocial attitudes or poor life skills, that brought them to this stage in the first place.

Monitor Compliance

Probation and parole officers apply several specific surveillance techniques to monitor offenders' compliance with court/parole board-ordered conditions. Examples are provided in Table 5.

In Robert's case monitoring techniques for the condition "obtain full-time employment, approved schooling or a full-time combination of both" could include: verification of job seeking activities through discussions with Robert, Mrs. Davis, and potential employers; a written assessment report and periodic progress reports from the vocational training program; drug and alcohol testing; and verification of Robert's performance of community service through weekly contact with Robert and his supervisor at the community service site.

In *"Restructuring Intensive Supervision Programs: Applying 'What Works'"* APPA (1994a) recommended that surveillance be conducted through constructive activities aimed at encouraging and monitoring progress in intervention components rather than mere supervision contacts. Focusing on limited and relevant conditions of probation and parole such as employment, involvement in an educational program, or substance abuse treatment does not mean that offenders will be watched less closely (Petersilia, Peterson & Turner, 1992). When officers are actively involved in the provision of services to offenders, they are in fact monitoring, surveilling, and controlling the offender under their supervision and can effectively enforce court/parole board-ordered sanctions.

Respond to Compliance/Noncompliance

The enforcement of established supervisory conditions is critical to the credibility of the court/parole board and community corrections agencies. Overlooking violations can lead to an offenders' loss of respect for probation/ parole officers and undermine the supervision process (Sutherland & Cressey, 1966). This reinforces the need for supervisory conditions to be "reasonably related to the avoidance of further criminal behavior and not unduly restrictive" (APPA, 1991, p. IX-7). The enforcement of court/parole board-ordered conditions requires

Table 4 - Facilitating Compliance through Individual Supervision Strategies

OFFENDER	IDENTIFIED PROBLEM(s)	SUPERVISION STRATEGY
Sam	• lack of job skills • low reading ability • poor interpersonal skills • no employment history • poor hygiene	• refer to job readiness classes and monitor progress • refer to adult basic education for reading improvement • assist offender in identifying jobs to apply for and with the completion of applications
Robert	• alcohol abuse • lack of motivation	• refer to drug/alcohol assessment and follow through with recommended treatment • refer to vocational assessment and follow-through with recommendations • require offender to apply for a minimum of three jobs per week • require verification of job seeking activities • order offender to perform 25 hours of community service per week until employment/schooling is obtained

Table 5 - Monitoring Court/Parole-Board Ordered Conditions

CONDITION	MONITORING TECHNIQUE
Obey all laws including federal, state, city and county laws.	• record checks • collateral contacts with law enforcement agencies • contacts with offender
Do not change residence without promptly informing the Probation/Parole Department or its representatives.	• electronic monitoring • home visits • collateral contacts with family • contacts with offender
Find and obtain gainful full-time employment, approved schooling or a full-time combination of both.	• verification of employment through pay stubs • contact with employers/schools • contacts with offender
Do not possess or consume any illegal substances.	• contact with treatment providers • drug/alcohol testing • observation through office/home contacts • collateral contacts with family/neighbors

two major components: 1) positive reinforcement for encouraging continued compliance and progress; and 2) a range of sanctions for responding to non-compliance and holding offenders accountable for their behavior.

While not typically thought of as an enforcement technique, positive reinforcement is a very potent mechanism for promoting positive behavioral change (Gendreau, 1994), and therefore, plays an important role in the enforcement of court/parole board-ordered conditions. Once a desired behavior or pattern of compliance is

exhibited, a common response from probation/parole officers is to reduce the level of restrictions, or requirements, placed on offenders. For example, if Robert becomes actively involved in a vocational program, or becomes gainfully employed, community service requirements may be reduced or eliminated. Often the number of supervisory contacts are reduced when an offender displays a pattern of compliance or prosocial behavior for a specified period of time. These positive responses reinforce an offenders' prosocial behavior and reduce their level of risk, both of which are important objectives of court/parole board-ordered conditions.

The more commonly identified enforcement technique is the application of a sanction in response to non-compliance. This, too, is a critical component of community corrections' ability to enforce court/parole board-ordered conditions. To maintain program credibility, and to hold offenders accountable for their actions, a wide range of responses must be available to probation/parole officers, including revocation and incarceration. More importantly, sanctions provide a mechanism for controlling the offender in the community and for protecting the public. Sanctioning options typically include:

- verbal reprimands;
- an increased level of supervisory contacts;
- increased drug or alcohol testing;
- community service requirements;
- curfews;
- house arrest;
- electronic monitoring;
- short-term detention; and
- revocation.

Many agencies include more intensive levels of intervention (e.g., inpatient drug/alcohol treatment) among their range of intermediate sanctions.

Responses to non-compliance should, ideally, be directly related to the nature of the violation and the level of risk that it poses to the community. Offenders' individual risks and needs should also be taken into consideration when imposing a sanction. In Robert's case, if drug and alcohol use is interfering with vocational training or job hunting, then perhaps a more intensive level of treatment should be required; if lack of motivation or responsibility appears to be the problem, the number of community service hours could be increased.

Varying levels of discretion are given to probation/parole officers in regards to reporting and responding to violations of court/parole board-ordered conditions. Many judges/parole board members want a formal notification of each violation that occurs, and prefer to determine the action(s) to be taken themselves. Others, however, leave it to the discretion of officers or their supervisors to determine when to file a formal petition and the appropriate response to violations.

Performance-Based Measures

Probation and parole agencies are responsible for facilitating, monitoring and enforcing court/parole board-orders, and for reporting non-compliance through appropriate channels. The following performance-based measures are designed to assess the degree to which officers are effective in fulfilling this critical responsibility. Process measures such as those provided below can assist agencies in determining if specific policies regarding the enforcement of court/parole board-ordered sanctions are being properly implemented. Outcome measures can be used to ascertain such results as the extent to which these policies promote compliance or lead to successful discharges from supervision.

Process Measures

Timely Imposition of Sanctions. Each time a violation is detected, officers must assess the situation and impose an appropriate sanction. Factors to consider include the offender's behavioral pattern and the level of risk that the current violating behavior creates. It is recommended that the least intrusive sanction be imposed that will decrease the negative behavior and increase prosocial behavior.

Timely responses to violations of supervisory conditions are necessary for maintaining program integrity. Furthermore, to be effective,

Figure 33 - Timely Imposition of Sanctions

Objective: During the first quarter of 1994, officers will impose a sanction within five working days of a positive urinalysis result 90% of the time.

Data Elements: Number of positive urinalyses, dates of positive urinalyses, dates sanctions were imposed.

Formula: Number of positive urinalyses in which a sanction was imposed within five working days ÷ total number of positive urinalyses x 100.

Example: During the first quarter of 1994, there were 536 positive urinalyses. A sanction was imposed within five working days of 402 of these positive results.

$402 \div 536 \times 100 = 75\%$ **Objective was not achieved.**

Figure 34 - Number of Revocation Proceedings Resulting from Technical Violations

Objective: The number of revocation hearings, solely for technical violations, will be reduced by five percent (5%) for FY 1994.

Data Elements: Total number of revocation hearings, number of revocation hearings for technical violations.

Formula: (Number of revocation hearings for technical violations ÷ total number of revocation hearings) x 100.

Example: During the first quarter of 1994, there were 145 revocation hearings. 38 of the hearings were based only on technical violations. During the fourth quarter of 1994, there were 189 revocation hearings. 43 of the hearings were based only on technical violations.

$(38 \div 145) \times 100 = 26\%$ for 1st Quarter

$(43 \div 189) \times 100 = 23\%$ for 4th Quarter

Objective was not achieved.

punishment (i.e., sanctions) must be administered immediately after the behavior has occurred (Gendreau, 1994). In the example provided, the agency has decided to focus on the timely imposition of sanctions in response to positive urinalyses as a means of deterring and reducing drug use. Similar objectives could be established for any violation of probation or parole.

Number of Petitions Filed for Technical Violations. Agency policies and procedures determine the extent of officer discretion in deciding when formal technical violations are filed. If officers have broad discretionary powers, the action taken in response to violations is often influenced by the officer's degree of tolerance. For example, Officer A may file a formal petition for revocation every time an offender has a positive urinalysis. Officer B, on the other hand, may examine the offender's

individual circumstances and thoroughly explore alternative interventions before deciding to file a formal petition on a similar offense. For an agency encouraging the exhaustive exploration of progressive interventions prior to filing a petition, a reduction in the number of petitions filed for technical violations alone could serve as one indicator of officers' effectiveness in facilitating, monitoring and enforcing court/parole board-sanctions.

Outcome Measures

Number and Type of Technical Violations. Outcome data on the number and type of techni-

Figure 35 - Reduction in Drug Use Violations

Objective: The number of drug use violations as detected by urinalysis will decrease by 10% during the second quarter of 1994 for offenders assigned to the ISP unit in the fourth quarter of 1993 (Group D).

Data elements: Number of offenders in Group D during fourth quarter of 1993, number of positive urinalyses among Group D during the fourth quarter of 1993, number of offenders remaining in Group D in second quarter of 1994, number of positive urinalyses among Group D during the second quarter of 1994.

Formula: ((Number of positive urinalyses for Group D during the 4th quarter of 1993 ÷ number of offenders in Group D) x 100 = % of drug use violations for Group D during the 4th quarter of 1993) - ((number of positive urinalyses for Group D during the 2nd quarter of 1994 ÷ number of offenders remaining in Group D) x 100) = % increase/ decrease in drug use violation among Group D.

Example: During the fourth quarter of 1993 there were 78 positive urinalyses among the 409 offenders in Group D. During the second quarter of 1994 there were 43 positive urinalyses among the 398 offenders remaining in Group D.

((78 ÷ 409) x 100) - ((31 ÷ 398) x 100) = 11% reduction in drug use among Group D. **Objective was achieved.**

---

cal violations may provide valuable information about which conditions are difficult to enforce, and shed light on potential reasons for this difficulty. A reduction in a specific type of violation (e.g., drug use) may reflect improved practices in this area (e.g., expanded or im-

proved treatment programs; increased deterrence from more frequent drug testing). All of these outcomes should be considered within the context of judicial/parole board practices and other agency policies to avoid a misinterpretation of the findings. Shifts in philosophies and practices could lead to the increased detection of violations or changes in reporting requirements. For example, if an agency implements an intensive supervision program, the number of technical violations detected will probably increase because of the heightened level of supervision. Under these circumstances, an uninformed stakeholder could misinterpret the increased level of technical violations as an increase in noncompliant behavior or a failure in enforcement strategies rather than a logical result of modified practices.

Percent of Community Service Performed. Community service is often included as a supervisory condition of probation/parole through the initial court/parole board orders or as a sanction in response to a violation. The extent to which this community service is actually performed is an indicator of the degree to which it is monitored and enforced.

This outcome measure is valuable for other reasons as well. The general public, a major stakeholder in the process, is often interested in how the offender is "paying a debt to society." The number of hours of community service performed satisfies this interest.

The total hours of community service performed during a specific period of time is one method for reporting this data. Reporting the percentage of community service performed compared to the amount of community service ordered actually provides a truer assessment of monitoring and enforcement strategies. Another reporting option involves the assignment of a dollar value to the number of community service hours performed; this measure communicates the value of a community service program in terms everyone understands. In the example provided, 2730 hours of community service valued at $5.00 per hour equals a total value of $13,650.

Figure 36 - Percent of Community Service Performed

Objective: 70% of all community service hours ordered during the first quarter of 1994 will be performed by the end of the fourth quarter of 1994.

Data Elements: Number of community service hours ordered during the first quarter of 1994, number of community service hours performed by the end of the fourth quarter of 1994.

Formula: (Number of community service hours performed by the end of the fourth quarter of 1994 ÷ number of community service hours ordered during the first quarter of 1994) x 100.

Example: 3500 hours of community service were ordered during the first quarter of 1994. 2730 hours were performed by the end of the fourth quarter of 1994.

(2730 ÷ 3500) x 100 = 78% of all community service hours ordered during the first quarter of 1994 were performed by the end of the fourth quarter of 1994. **Objective was achieved.**

Reporting on the amount and percentage of community service hours performed is just one example of an outcome measure that can be used to demonstrate the level of compliance with specific court/parole board orders. Similar measures could be used for assessing the level of compliance with orders regarding participation in educational or employment programming or payment of financial obligations. A high level

of noncompliance of one type should cause agencies to examine related practices.

Percent of Favorable Discharges. A favorable discharge indicates that the offender has "satisfied" court/parole board obligations. The extent to which all court/parole-ordered sanctions have been met prior to discharge from supervision often varies due to individual offender circumstances. If an officer believes that supervisory obligations have been fulfilled to the best of the offender's ability and that the offender has received maximum benefit from supervision, then a favorable discharge is often granted regardless of whether or not each condition was

Figure 37 - Percent of Favorable Discharges

Objective: 80% of all offenders terminated from parole supervision during FY 1994 will receive favorable discharges.

Data Elements: Number of offenders terminated from parole supervision during 1994 receiving favorable discharges, total number of offenders terminated from parole supervision during 1994.

Formula: (Number of offenders terminated from parole supervision during 1994 receiving favorable discharges ÷ total number of offenders terminated from parole supervision during 1994) x 100

Example: 350 offenders were terminated from parole supervision during 1994. 236 of these offenders received favorable discharges.

(236 ÷ 350) x 100 = 67% of offenders terminated from parole supervision received favorable discharges. **Objective was not achieved.**

---

met. For these reasons, the percent of favorable discharges should be combined with other outcome measures addressed in this chapter. For example, eighty-five percent of the offenders granted a favorable discharge from supervision completed all community service requirements; 79 percent were gainfully employed; and 70 percent of those offenders without a high school diploma or GED, obtained a GED. Other educational and treatment activities could be reported to demonstrate that the department is making reasonable efforts to rehabilitate the offenders and return them as productive members of society.

Conclusion

As discussed throughout this chapter, enforcement requires much more than the application of sanctions to noncompliance. Probation and parole officers are responsible for facilitating compliance through problem-solving approaches and interventions, and for monitoring compliance through various mechanisms of surveillance and community contacts. A common criticism of community corrections is that probation/parole are just "slaps on the wrist." Process measures can provide this skeptical audience with evidence that offenders are being held accountable for their crimes through the imposition and enforcement of conditions aimed at controlling them in the community and producing law-abiding behavior. Outcome measures assist agencies in evaluating the effectiveness of these strategies and guide the development or improvement of enforcement practices. Consistent monitoring and improvement is essential since policies and practices associated with the enforcement of court/parole board-ordered sanctions are directly related to those designed to protect the community and assist offenders to change as will be discussed in the chapters that follow.

CHAPTER FIVE

PROTECT THE COMMUNITY

> **GOAL:** The Anytown, USA Community Corrections Department will protect the community through appropriate assessment, intervention, surveillance and enforcement activities.

Introduction

Protecting the community is an indisputable component of community corrections' mission. While professionals may argue about whether or not community corrections is in the business of behavioral change or about the extent of services to be provided to courts and parole boards, few will argue about whether or not protecting the community should be a driving force behind program development and operations within community corrections. It is the activities performed in the name of protecting the community and the measures of success that create discomfort and disagreement. This chapter will explore common strategies for achieving community protection, specific activities conducted to protect the community, and a framework for measuring success as it relates to this crucial mission component.

Rationale for Goal

Protecting the community has always been, and continues to be a primary objective of the criminal justice system. As the number of offenders under some form of community supervision escalates, the role of community corrections in meeting that objective becomes even more crucial. Throughout the literature three basic strategies for protecting the community are discussed: deterrence, incapacitation, and rehabilitation.

The principle of deterrence claims that punishment will reduce crime by creating specific deterrence for the individual experiencing the punishment; and general deterrence for others who observe the punishment (Shichor, 1992). A problem with this simple concept, the prevention of future criminal activity by showing that the price exacted for committing crimes is greater than the gain (Palmer, 1992), lies in basing "assumptions about what punishes on the norms and living standards of society at large" (Petersilia, 1990, p. 23). What is perceived as punishment by prosocial citizens may be seen as the "cost of doing business" for offenders whose values and beliefs differ. This is best illustrated by the failure of mandatory sentencing laws to reduce the number and severity of drug offenses (Edna McConnell-Clark Foundation, 1993).

Incapacitation is thought by many to be the only sure way to achieve public safety; "if you can't change people, you can certainly control them" (O'Leary, 1987). Incapacitation renders further offenses impossible by placing the offender in jail or prison (Palmer, 1992). This was the leading penal principle in the 1980s which led to the prison crowding crisis (Shichor, 1992). Because of the crowded prisons and the exorbitant costs it became necessary to find a way to control offenders within the community (Clear & Hardyman, 1990). Various forms of community corrections emerged, most notably intensive supervision programs and electronic monitoring. To gain credibility, these programs were based on incapacitative principles with strict surveillance and tight controls imposed within the community.

Rehabilitation, as a strategy for achieving public safety, has ebbed and flowed throughout the history of the criminal justice system. Rehabilitation focuses on individual offenders and seeks to reduce recidivism through interventions aimed at changing offenders' attitudes and behaviors (Sechrest et al., 1979). Rehabilitative interventions are designed to effect long-term cures of crime and delinquency even after the offender is released from supervision, rather than to provide short-term suppression of the symptoms (Harland & Rosen, 1987). Under this theory, probation and parole officers act as counselors and advocates (Lawrence, 1991). It is their job to diagnose the problem that contributes to the offender's criminal behavior and provide services that may resolve it (Petersilia & Turner, 1990). From a political perspective, rehabilitative strategies are often viewed as being "soft on crime." An emerging body of research (Byrne & Kelly, 1989; Petersilia & Turner, 1993; Cullen & Gendreau, 1988; Gendreau & Andrews, 1990), however, suggests that effective rehabilitative programming offers a promising avenue for achieving public safety objectives. Of 443 rehabilitation programs reviewed, the average reduction in recidivism was ten percent (Lipsey, 1990 as cited in Gendreau, 1994), and those programs that applied certain principles of effective intervention demonstrated reductions in recidivism, on the average, of fifty percent (Gendreau, 1994). Positive outcomes such as these are keeping the rehabilitation agenda alive.

Retribution is another common strategy applied throughout the Criminal Justice System. Retrib-

utive strategies are seen as more expressive than utilitarian. Retribution is "punishment for the sake of punishment" (Palmer, 1992, p. vii). In a retributive model, an individual's past conduct and the instant offense are the determining factors in the sentence imposed rather than predictions and beliefs about the propensity to reoffend (von Hirsch, 1976; Harris, 1984). Within this context, the helping or service role is seen as inappropriate; the sanction is based on what the offender *did*, not on what he or she *might* do (Harris, 1984). The "just deserts" model of corrections, so popular over the past few decades, emphasizes retributive and "deserved" punishments (Benekos, 1990). According to the Uniform Crime Report, the crime rate has increased steadily since 1980, and there are more people in the nation's prisons than ever before (Edna McConnell-Clark Foundation, 1993).

How effectively these different strategies are in achieving public safety is still unclear; partly because of the difficulty in disentangling the effects of these strategies and techniques and partly because of the difficulties associated with measuring public safety. Perhaps the trouble lies, not within the strategies, but within the nebulous definitions of community protection. As demonstrated below, varying interpretations of public safety appear within the literature.

• Comparisons of recidivism rates for prison releasees with those placed in community corrections programs often reveal "no significant differences." Criminal justice researchers and practitioners use this information to indicate the achievement of public safety objectives, claiming that they at least did not threaten public safety (Erwin & Bennett, 1987; Wagner & Baird, 1993).

• Many practitioners suggest that the research showing no significant reductions in recidivism for ISP offenders (and therefore no increased public safety) is deceptive; the recidivism rates reported include those offenders who are returned to prison for technical violations. These practitioners argue that removing offenders from the streets because of technical violations pre-empts criminal behavior and therefore increases public safety (Wagner, 1989; Nidorf, 1991).

- O'Leary and Clear (1984) suggest that public safety is achieved by controlling offender risk. "Conditions of probation and parole required of the offender are designed to minimize the likelihood of future criminal acts" (p. 1).

- A study of a New York Boot Camp revealed that recidivism rates for boot camp participants, 12 months after their release, were lower than those of a comparison group of inmates. However, the differences in recidivism rates tend to decrease over time (United States General Accounting Office [GAO], 1993).

Is the community protected when community corrections "suppresses criminal behavior by pre-empting it with technical violations?" Does the fact that community corrections offenders "do no worse" than prison releasees represent public safety? Is community protection achieved through "the minimization of the likelihood" of an offender committing future acts? Does the negligible long-term impact on recidivism rates by the New York boot camp suggest that public safety objectives were not achieved? The intention here is not to suggest a correct answer to any of these questions, but to encourage their exploration. The first step in determining how to measure "protecting the community" is to clearly define what it means to the agency.

One step toward making this determination is to ask the consumers (i.e., the community) of the product (i.e., protection; safety) for their percep-

tions and expectations. In an article, "Alternative Sentencing: Selling it to the Public," Delaware Governor Michael N. Castle states "it is people's perception of their personal safety as well as allocation of their hard-earned money that you must address" (Castle, 1991). Public opinion polls suggest that policy makers vastly overrate the public's desire for punishment (Doble, 1987; Cullen, Cullen & Wozniak, 1988; Tilow, 1992). What the public seems to want is public safety and, once educated on the costs and benefits of various strategies for achieving public safety, there is a high level of support for alternatives to punishment and incarceration (Doble, 1987). It may benefit community corrections to find out what makes people feel safe, and to educate them on the role that community corrections can play in that safety. The collaborative establishment of reasonable expectations will result in meaningful program activities and outcome measures that accurately assess the effectiveness of community corrections in protecting the community.

Probation and Parole Activities

"While it is easy to specify that correctional managers should not take actions that jeopardize the safety of the community, translating this aim into action is not simple, for the best method to protect the public is not always clear" (O'Leary & Clear, 1984, p. 5). Evidence of this statement can be found in the major theoretical and operational shifts that have occurred throughout the past several decades. Since the early 1960s, the activities performed under the guise of protecting the community have changed from offender-oriented programs in which rehabilitation was the primary emphasis, and enforcement of conditions was secondary, to societally-oriented programs grounded in punishment and incapacitation (Cochran, Corbett, & Byrne, 1986; Lipchitz, 1986; O'Leary, 1987; Byrne, 1989; Benekos, 1990). As the knowledge base on effective correctional programming expands, agencies are choosing an *integrated approach* of interventions and risk-control strategies to achieve public safety. It is important to differentiate between techniques designed to promote long-term behavioral change and those that provide short-term crime control, and to recognize the importance of having both to protecting the community. The case example provided in Chapter Four, Robert Davis, will be used to illustrate this point.

The activities discussed below are generally conducted on each offender to determine what services and risk-control strategies are likely to produce law abiding behavior and to monitor the effectiveness of those strategies. Clearly, diverse offender characteristics would dictate the use of varying strategies for protecting the community. A generic discussion on each activity and its relationship to community protection will be followed by an example of how these activities are applied to the specific case of Robert Davis.

Risk/Need Assessment

Initial risk/need assessment provides a basis for case classification. Case classification "consists of a set of guidelines that specifically attempt to link offenders with the clinical and administrative decisions of the probation or parole officer" (Gendreau, 1994). Essential to the case classification process is the ability to make decisions about the offender's future behavior based on past and present factors. These factors are defined in terms of risks and needs. Risks are measurable attributes of offenders and their situations which are predictive of future adjustment while under supervision or after the supervisory period has terminated. These risks are either static or dynamic in nature. Static factors are those fixed in time (e.g., age and number of previous convictions). While good predictors of recidivism, a probation/parole officer is powerless to affect change in these areas. Needs are

dynamic factors that are changeable. An offender's level of substance abuse, attitudes toward work and authority figures, and educational status are three such examples (Gendreau, 1994). It is essential that these criminogenic needs are assessed and targeted for change as a means to protect the community. If prosocial changes occur in these areas, the likelihood that the offender will become reinvolved in criminal activity is reduced.

There are two ways by which risk is determined. One method is the "clinical" approach whereby the person carrying out the assessment does so from their own personal, theoretical framework based on intuition and subjective judgement. The other approach, one that has proven over thirty years of research to be the more reliable and accurate, is the "actuarial" model (Glaser, 1987; Clear & O'Leary, 1983; and Andrews, Bonta & Hoge, 1990). Actuarial models base their predictions on objective, standardized, and empirical measures of risk. A variety of standardized assessment instruments are used across the nation. The most widely used risk assessment tool in the United States is the Wisconsin model or a variation thereof. This basic model uses two separate scales; one for assessing risks and one for assessing needs. Other instruments include both measures on one scale. The following example assesses the risks and needs of Robert Davis.

RISK ASSESSMENT OF ROBERT DAVIS

SCORE

1. NUMBER OF ADDRESS CHANGES IN LAST 12 MONTHS:

0 None
2 One
3 Two or more   **2**

2. TIME EMPLOYED IN LAST 12 MONTHS: . . . .

0 More than 8 months
1 4 to 7 months
2 Under 4 months
0 Not applicable   **2**

3. ALCOHOL USAGE PROBLEMS: . . . .

0 No interference with functioning
2 Some disruption of functioning
4 Serious disruption; needs treatment   **4**

4. OTHER DRUG USAGE PROBLEMS: . . . .

0 No usage of illegal drugs
1 Occasional use
2 Frequent use; needs treatment   **1**

5. ATTITUDE: . . . .

0 Motivated to change; receptive
  to assistance
3 Dependent or unwilling to accept responsibility
5 Rationalizes behavior; negative;
  not motivated to change   **5**

6. AGE AT FIRST CONVICTION: . . . .
   (or Juvenile Adjudication in the last 5 years)

0 24 or older
2 20-23
4 19 or younger   **4**

7. NUMBER OF PRIOR PERIODS OF PROBATION/PAROLE
   SUPERVISION: . . . .
   (Adult or Juvenile)

0 None
2 One
4 Two or more   **2**

8. NUMBER OF PRIOR PROBATION/PAROLE REVOCATIONS:
   (Adult or Juvenile)

0 None
4 One or more   **0**

9. NUMBER OF PRIOR FELONY CONVICTIONS: . . . .
   (or Juvenile Adjudications in the last 5 years)

0 None
2 One
4 Two or more   **0**

10. ADULT CONVICTIONS/JUVENILE ADJUDICATIONS FOR: .
    (Select applicable offenses and add for score. Do not
    exceed a total of 5. Include current offense.)

0 Not applicable
2 Burglary, theft, auto theft, or
  robbery
3 Worthless checks or forgery   **0**

11. ADULT CONVICTIONS/JUVENILE ADJUDICATIONS FOR
    ASSAULTIVE OFFENSE WITHIN LAST FIVE YEARS: . . . .

15 Yes
0 No   **15**

    (An offense which involves the use of a
    weapon, physical force, or the threat of force.)

TOTAL RISK SCORE   **35**

NEEDS ASSESSMENT OF ROBERT DAVIS

								SCORE
1.	ACADEMIC/ VOCA-TIONAL SKILLS	0	Adequate skills; able to handle everyday requirements	+2	Low skill level causing minor adjustment problems	+4	Minimum skill level causing serious adjustment problems	2
2.	EMPLOYMENT	0	Secure employment; no difficulties reported; or homemaker, student or retired	+3	Unsatisfactory employment; or unemployed but has adequate job skills	+6	Unemployed and virtually unemployable; needs training	3
3.	FINANCIAL MANAGEMENT	0	No current difficulties	+3	Situational or minor difficulties	+5	Severe difficulties; may include garnishment, bad checks or bankruptcy	3
4.	MARITAL/FAMILY RELATIONSHIPS	0	Relatively stable relationships	+3	Some disorganization or stress but potential for improvement	+5	Major disorganization or stress	5
5.	COMPANIONS	0	No adverse relationships	+2	Association with occasional negative results	+4	Associations negative	4
6.	EMOTIONAL STABILITY	0	No symptoms of emotional instability; appropriate emotional responses	+4	Symptoms limited but do not prohibit adequate functioning; e.g., excessive anxiety	+7	Symptoms prohibit adequate functioning; e.g., lashes out or retreats into self	7
7.	ALCOHOL USAGE	0	No interference with functioning	+3	Occasional abuse; some disruption of functioning	+6	Frequent abuse; serious disruption; needs treatment	6
8.	OTHER DRUG USAGE	0	No interference with functioning	+3	Occasional substance use; some disruption of functioning	+5	Frequent substance use; serious disruption; needs treatment	3
9.	LEARNING ABILITY	0	Able to function independently	+3	Some need for assistance; potential for adequate adjustment	+6	Deficiencies severely limit independent functioning	0
10.	HEALTH	0	Sound physical health; seldom ill	+1	Handicap or illness interferes with functioning on a recurring basis	+2	Serious handicap or chronic illness; needs frequent medical care	0
11.	SEXUAL BEHAVIOR	0	No apparent dysfunction	+3	Real or perceived situational or minor problems	+5	Real or perceived chronic or severe problems	0
12.	OFFICER'S IMPRESSION OF CLIENT'S NEEDS	0	Minimum	+3	Medium	+5	Maximum	5

TOTAL NEED SCORE   **38**

Figure 38 - Classifications

Level of Supervision	Risk Score	Need Score
Maximum	18 and above	30 and above
Medium	7 to 17	15 to 29
Minimum	6 and below	14 and below

Once the instruments are completed, offenders are assigned to the highest level of supervision indicated on the risk/need scale (see Figure 38). As can be seen, Robert Davis' assessment scores would place him in a maximum level of supervision. The assessment indicates that Robert has many criminogenic needs that should be addressed. His primary areas of need are: 1) emotional stability; 2) marital/family relationships; and 3) alcohol abuse. Secondary areas of need include employment, academic/vocational skills, financial management, companions and drug use. Robert's classification suggests that he requires maximum levels of supervision and services aimed at addressing the identified needs, controlling his criminal behavior, and holding him accountable for his actions.

Actuarial risk/need assessments are designed to identify factors associated with an offender's criminal behavior. They provide a quantitative measurement of an offender's likelihood of reoffending. They serve as one source of information for allocating resources and for developing case plans aimed at controlling risks and addressing needs as means to protect the community from further criminal acts. A more indepth assessment may be required to more clearly determine Robert's needs and the appropriate services for meeting those needs. Additional assessment strategies will be discussed further in Chapter Six.

Case Planning

Case planning is a comprehensive process beginning with assessment and ending with monitoring and evaluation. Clear and O'Leary (1983) specify four critical steps in the case planning process including: 1) risk classification (as described above); 2) analysis of key forces; 3) specification of objectives; and 4) specification of resources. The latter three steps will be discussed briefly to demonstrate how the case planning process contributes to the goal of protecting the community.

Once the risks are identified a case plan must be formulated that will control or reduce those risks. Because of resource and time constraints for both offenders and officers it is necessary to prioritize problems and focus first on those areas most strongly associated with the offender's criminal behavior. This can be accomplished through the second step in the case planning process, conducting a *force-field analysis*. Clear & O'Leary (1983) adapted the *force-field analysis*, as developed by Kurt Lewin, to identify the forces *driving* law abiding behavior and the forces *restricting* law abiding behavior which exist in an offender's life. A force-field analysis on Robert Davis appears in Figure 39.

One way to look at case planning, then, is to develop methods to alter these forces in order to increase the chances of an offender engaging in law abiding behavior.

Figure 39 - Force Field Analysis for Robert Davis

Forces Driving for More Law-Abiding Behavior ------>	Forces Restricting <------Law-Abiding Behavior
1. Likable	1. Alcohol/drug abuse
2. Displays periods of motivation	2. Impulsivity
3. Aptitude for carpentry work	3. Family instability
4. Normal intelligence	4. Relationship problems
5. Generally in good physical health	5. 10th grade education
	6. Unstable employment history
	7. History of assaultive behavior
	8. Negative companions

Once identified, Clear and O'Leary (1983) offer four guidelines for prioritizing these forces:

1) Strength - forces that are important in determining the frequency of an event;

2) Alterability - forces where existing means are available to change the degree or nature of their influence on the event;

3) Speed - forces that can be quickly manipulated; and

4) Interdependency - forces that are crucial because a change in them will influence many other forces.

Based upon these criteria, Robert's initial case plan should focus on two key target areas: 1) alcohol/drug abuse; and 2) emotional instability.

Robert's alcohol abuse is clearly a strong contributor to his criminal activity and requires immediate and long-term attention. Alcohol abuse is likely to interfere with his emotional stability and, specifically, his ability to control his anger. Robert's alcohol abuse and his emotional instability have interfered with his employment and his family relationships, and most significantly, have contributed to domestic violence. Altering these key forces will influence many other forces and increase Robert's chances for law-abiding behavior. Improvement in both of these target areas, however, will require long-term efforts. In addition to developing a case plan to address the two primary areas of need, an officer may choose to establish objectives aimed at improving Robert's vocational skills or employment. Quick progress may be possible in this area and provide both the offender and the officer with a sense of accomplish-

Figure 40 - Initial Case Plan for Robert Davis

Behavioral Objectives	Importance of Objective	Resource
1) To function appropriately in society without using drugs and alcohol for the next three months.	Critical	Probation Officer Anytown Mental Health Center AA
2) To participate in treatment for domestic violence for the next three months.	Critical	Safe Place, Inc. Probation Officer
3) To set up and attend an evaluation concerning educational and voca-	Important	Vocational Rehabilitation

ment. Furthermore, participation in vocational training or employment will structure Robert's time and reduce his opportunities for becoming involved in antisocial behavior.

The third step in the case planning process involves specifying behavioral objectives for the offender to achieve throughout the period of supervision. It is recommended that these objectives be established through a joint, problem-solving approach between the officer and the offender to increase the offender's commitment to the case plan. Behavioral objectives should be designed to focus the offender and the officer on the desired outcomes, and allow for review, modification, and improvements to the case plan. The fourth step in the case planning process involves specifying the resources to be used in accomplishing supervision objectives. Figure 40 includes an objectives-based case plan designed to begin addressing Robert's primary needs.

The utility of the objectives-based case plan is obvious. It provides concrete, attainable milestones for the offender and guides the supervision process toward the goals of the organization; in this case protection of the community. Case plans, such as the one developed for Robert Davis should be viewed as dynamic plans requiring ongoing review and modification based on the offender's progress. The next two sections outline methods for implementing the case plan and for measuring the effectiveness of the supervision provided.

Case Supervision

To implement the case plan, community corrections must provide the full range of probation and parole activities designed to meet the objectives of risk-control and public safety. These activities and objectives can generally be categorized as *intervention, surveillance* and *enforcement*. Within this context, *intervention* includes the entire range of treatment and services provided to offenders including drug/alcohol treatment, job skills training, mental health counseling, and GED classes. Recent research suggests that the provision of treatment and services is an effective means of control and behavioral reform by holding offenders strictly accountable for their actions (Gendreau & Andrews, 1990; Gendreau & Ross, 1987). In Robert's case, treatment and services to be provided include drug/alcohol treatment, group therapy for domestic violence, and vocational assessment and training.

Surveillance involves those activities which relate to monitoring offender activity as well as the social environment of the offender. The importance of monitoring the social milieu rests on the potential positive/negative effect on the offender of factors such as family problems or shifts in employment trends. Surveillance tools include home visits, contacts with employers, neighborhood contacts, and electronic monitoring. To monitor Robert's progress, the officer could conduct urinalysis, maintain contact with the treatment providers, require verification of attendance, and discuss Robert's progress and compliance with the case plan with him and his family members.

The *enforcement* component speaks to the need to hold offenders strictly accountable for their actions. To meet this need there must be a wide range of options available, including custody. Enforcement options could include verbal reprimands, increased levels of supervision, community service requirements, curfew, house arrest, or short-term incarceration. Depending on the offenders' level of risk, various enforcement strategies may be required initially as part of the supervisory conditions. As an offender progresses, these conditions should be reduced. Likewise, a lack of progress should drive the application of more stringent enforcement strategies. In Robert's case, noncompliance would require a stringent response such as house arrest or short-term detention since a lack of progress could contribute to further violent behavior.

Intervention, surveillance, and enforcement are the conceptual frameworks within which probation and parole can address the public's concern for the risk of conditionally released offenders. A firm, fair and accountable approach can provide short-term control of offenders and long-term behavioral reform, both of which are essential to public safety objectives.

Risk/Need Reassessment

Measuring change in the level of offenders' risks/needs through periodic reassessment is essential to the goal of protecting the community for three primary reasons. First, an important task of community corrections is to manage offenders in such a way that low risk cases remain low risk, and high risk offenders move into lower risk categories (Andrews, 1989). Periodic reassessment allows officers to monitor changes in an offender's risks/needs to ascertain if they are accomplishing this task, and to assess the effectiveness of the supervision provided. Second, reassessment allows officers to adjust clinical and administrative decisions in response to the changes in risk/need. "Once in the correctional system, offenders are subject to events and experiences that may produce shifts in their chances of recidivism" (Andrews, 1989). As offenders change so should the nature and level of supervision provided. This also allows agencies to allocate resources in such a way that those offenders presenting the most risk receive the highest levels of service. Third, measuring offender change can supplement an agency's knowledge about which factors are most strongly related to recidivism. Figure 41 depicts how offender change within a probation office in Ontario, Canada correlates with recidivism rates.

Figure 41 - Recidivism Rates by Changes in Problem Area

PROBLEM AREA OF PROBATIONER	RECIDIVISM RATES		
	No Change	Improvement	Worse
Drugs/alcohol	47%	39%	68%
Employment	43%	41%	61%
Hostility	49%	35%	72%
Leisure time	42%	35%	71%
Peer relations	46%	32%	63%
Schooling	43%	31%	48%
Self-efficacy	42%	30%	53%

Source: Gendreau, P. (1994a). Principles of effective intervention. In *Restructuring Intensive Supervision Programs: Applying "What Works."* Lexington, KY: American Probation and Parole Association.

To obtain this data, officers routinely measured change in the needs of their probationers each six months. As can be seen, those offenders who showed improvement in drugs/alcohol had a 39 percent recidivism rate compared with a 68 percent recidivism rate for those who worsened. This information provides powerful support for providing drug/alcohol services to offenders as a means for achieving public safety goals.

Risk/need reassessment completes the cyclical process that probation and parole agencies use to manage their offender population in an effort to reduce risk and protect the public. The next section will describe how monitoring outcomes related to this process can enhance an agency's ability to achieve this critical goal.

Performance-Based Measures

The primary outcome measure used by agencies to evaluate whether or not it has protected the community is recidivism. However, as discussed in Chapter One, recidivism rates alone provide very little information about which program components effectively reduce risk. They provide one dimensional information -- the offender was either arrested for a new crime or not. Process measures should be used to determine if appropriate case planning techniques are used to address offenders risks and needs and if intervention, surveillance, and enforcement strategies are implemented as designed. Additionally, intermediate outcome measures should be established to more accurately determine the degree to which various probation and parole activities reduce risk to communities. The remainder of this chapter discusses potential measures for evaluating the achievement of this goal.

Process Measures

Percent of Reassessments Conducted. Assessment of an offender's needs are a vital part of evaluating an offender's risk to the community. The results of the assessment are used to establish a case plan for the offender that meets the individual's needs, as well as, protects the community.

Figure 42 - Percent of Offenders Reassessed According to Agency Policies

---

Objective: 90% of all offenders will be reassessed at least once during each six-month period.

Data Elements: Number of offenders on supervision, number of offenders reassessed during a six-month period.

Formula: Number of offenders reassessed during a six-month period ÷ number of offenders on supervision x 100.

Example: During the first six months of 1994, there were 7127 offenders on supervision. 6984 offenders were reassessed during the period.

(6984 ÷ 7127) x 100 = 98% **Objective was achieved!!!**

The assessment results are a useful tool in the prediction of future activities, however, changes in the offender's circumstances, both positive and negative, limit the ability of the initial assessment to accurately predict future criminal activities. To provide current information on which to make changes in the case plan, reassessment of offenders should take place on a regular basis. Reassessment results could identify circumstances whereby the supervision level and/or activities could be reduced. On the other hand, reassessment results could identify circumstances that would dictate an increase in supervision activities to adequately protect the community.

The agency should have policies and procedures to guide a probation/parole officer in determining when reassessment activities are warranted. The goal of any evaluation of reassessment activities would be to determine if the agency's policies had been carried out.

Percent of Structured Time. Offender risks and needs should dictate the application of varying supervision strategies. Whether an offender is required to attend intensive outpatient treatment or ordered to serve a period of house arrest, a common objective is to involve the offender in activities in which they are held accountable for their whereabouts and can be monitored. Structured time serves an incapacitative purpose as it inhibits an offender's involvement in criminal activity. The average amount of structured time for offenders provides a good measure of an agency's attempts to protect the community. This process measure may be more suitable for intermediate sanction programs such as ISP or electronic monitoring since traditional supervision programs are typically unable to provide this level of structure.

Structured time can include:

- hours subject to house arrest;

- hours subject to a curfew;

- work hours;

- time in treatment programming; or

- hours of community service performed.

House arrest has become a more common strategy for controlling offenders within the communi-

Figure 43 - Percent of Structured Time

Objective: 60% of a high risk offender's time will be structured per week.

Data elements: Structured time per offender (number of hours subject to curfew, number of hours subject to house arrest, time in treatment, number of hours at work per week, number of hours in community service per week).

Formula: Structured time per offender ÷ no. of hours per week x 100

Example: John Jones works 40 hours per week, is subject to a curfew of 11 p.m. - 6 a.m. (7 hours per night), and attends three, one hour group sessions per week accounting for 55% of his weekly time.

92 ÷ 168 x 100 = 55%. **Objective was not achieved.**

ty with the advent of intermediate sanction programs. Additionally, many offenders in these programs are subject to a curfew. Documenting the number of offenders subject to house arrest or a curfew serves as an indicator of an agency's attempts to structure and monitor offenders' time. The high level of surveillance and monitoring required of high risk offenders should enable officers to verify the time spent in each of these activities. The failure to achieve the objective should drive corrective action. For example, John Jones' curfew could be changed to 9:00 p.m. or he could be required to perform community service or attend self-help groups, or a combination of all three.

Outcome Measures

Average Reduction in Risk/Need Levels. The basic premise of community corrections established in the previous section is that the combination of controls and services will reduce an offender's level of risk and need leading to enhanced public safety. An obvious outcome measure, then, is reduced levels of risk/need. This can be determined by comparing initial assessment scores with reassessment scores.

Figure 44 - Average Reduction in Risk/Need

Objective: Six month offender reassessments will reveal an average reduction in risk/need of 10%.

Data elements: Total sum of score differentials from initial to six month assessment for all offenders, total sum of initial scores for all offenders.

Formula: Total sum of score differentials from initial to six month assessment for all offenders ÷ total sum of initial scores for all offenders x 100.

Example: During 1994 the average reduction in risk/need from initial to six month reassessments was 12%.

2160 ÷ 18000 x 100 = 12% **Objective was achieved!**

This is a potent measurement of the effectiveness of the supervision provided.

A measurable reduction in risk provides strong documentation to support an agency's activities. Comparing such statistics across officers' caseloads (assuming all caseloads are equal) could provide insight regarding various supervision styles. Had the objective not been achieved, intervention programming would need to be examined to identify possible reasons for their failure to produce measurable changes.

Percentage of Positive Urinalyses. It has long been established that drug and alcohol

Figure 45 - Percentage of Positive Urinalyses

Objective: The percentage of positive urinalyses for offenders in the Specialized Drug Offender Program (SDOP) will not exceed 20% during FY 1994.

Data elements: Number of urinalyses conducted in SDOP during 1994, number of positive urinalyses for SDOP offenders in 1994.

Formula: (Number of positive urinalyses ÷ number urinalyses conducted) x 100.

Example: In January 1994, 2976 urinalyses were conducted on SDOP offenders. Of these, 844 were positive.

844 ÷ 2976 x 100 = 28%. **Objective was not achieved.**

---

abuse is strongly related to criminal behavior. Reduced rates of abuse can be documented through the use of urinalysis, and can demonstrate an agency's specific attempts to monitor offenders' progress in this area.

The failure to achieve the stated objective should guide agencies to explore several questions including: 1) Are treatment needs being appropriately identified? 2) Are offenders participating in treatment? 3) What treatment resources are being used? 4) Are sanctions being imposed following a positive urinalysis? The findings to these, and other questions, should drive program modifications.

Other possible outcome measures for monitoring drug/alcohol use and the effectiveness of related policies and programs include:

• reduced percentage of positive urinalyses among a specific subgroup of offenders; and

• the average number of days drug/alcohol free per offender.

To accurately measure the average number of days drug/alcohol free, it would be necessary to test each offender at least twice per week. An outcome measure of this nature may be best applied to those offenders with an identified addiction.

These types of measures should be taken one step further and examined within the context of recidivism rates. For example, the following chart relates improvements in drug and alcohol abuse, as measured by a reduction in positive urinalyses, to new arrests. As can be seen, those offenders showing reduced levels of drug/alcohol use had lower rates of new arrests.

	Improvement	No improvement
Rate of new arrest	12% (n = 43)	48% (n = 21)

This type of data has strong policy implications. It suggests that drug and alcohol treatment and testing provides a promising avenue for achieving public safety objectives. The goal of protecting the community is based on the premise that the supervision provided to offenders will reduce an offender's ability and motivation to become involved in further criminal activity. Most community corrections agencies track the number and type of new arrests. Because new arrests are only indicators of "officially recorded recidivism" the full extent of criminal activity by offenders is difficult to measure. Still, it is important to examine rates of new arrests and to discover if patterns exist by the type and level of supervision provided.

<u>Successful Completion of Treatment Orders</u>. Offenders are generally required to attend treatment or counseling programs to address factors contributing to their criminal activity. Successful completion of a treatment program is an indicator that the presenting need has been met

Figure 46 - Percent of Treatment Orders Completed

Objective: 75% of offenders with treatment orders will successfully complete their program during FY 1994.

Data elements: Number of offenders with treatment orders, number of offenders who successfully completed treatment orders.

Formula: Number of offenders who successfully completed treatment orders ÷ total number of offenders with treatment orders x 100.

Example: There were 926 treatment orders imposed. 769 of those were successfully completed.

(769 ÷ 926 = 83%). **Objective was achieved.**

(i.e., the offender has learned how to cope with anger; the offender has abstained from drug/alcohol abuse). Furthermore, studies have found a correlation between treatment retention and completion, and reduced recidivism (Jolin & Stipak, 1992). Therefore, a high rate of treatment completions would represent an attempt to reduce public risk.

In addition to the overall rate of treatment orders completed, the completion rate of specific types of treatment orders should be documented. Such information may reveal a deficiency in the mental health counseling offenders are receiving or the insufficient treatment provided in a particular drug/alcohol program. This information allows probation and parole agencies to take a more active role in ensuring that offenders are receiving effective treatment. It may also expose a failure to enforce treatment orders on the part of probation and parole personnel.

<u>Percent of Absconders During Supervision Period</u>. The rate of absconding is an obvious indicator of an agency's ability to fulfill its goal of protecting the community. If an offender's whereabouts are unknown, it is likely that the criminogenic needs are not being met and the likelihood of further criminal activity increases.

Figure 47 - Absconding Rate

Objective: The absconding rate for 1994 will not exceed 5%.

Data elements: Number of absconders, total number of offenders.

Formula: Number of absconders ÷ total number of offenders x 100.

Example: Of 7127 offenders, 213 were declared as absconders during 1994.

(213 ÷ 7127) x 100 = 3%. **Objective was achieved.**

A high absconding rate could be attributed to many factors including:

- a failure to gather a sufficient amount of information regarding the offender's living arrangements, family members, employment;

- an insufficient level of field and collateral contacts; or

- delayed responses to offenders' failure to report.

The exploration of possible contributing factors could lead to important program adjustments.

<u>Employment Rates</u>. Employment is also strongly related to recidivism. An agency can demonstrate their commitment to reducing public risk by measuring the percent of time employed

Figure 48 - Rate of Offender Employment

Objective: 65% of all offenders will maintain full-time (30 hours/week for 10 months) employment throughout 1994.

Data elements: Number of offenders working full-time, total number of offenders.

Formula: Number of offenders working full-time ÷ total number of offenders x 100.

Example: Of 7127 offenders, 5131 were employed for a minimum of 10 months at 30 hours per week.

(5131 ÷ 7127) x 100 = 72%. **Objective was achieved.**

Figure 49 - Percentage of Revocations Due to Technical Violations

Objective: Technical violations will account for 80% of revocations during 1994.

Data elements: Number of offenders with technical violations leading to revocation, total number of offenders revoked.

Formula: Number of offenders revoked for a technical violation ÷ total number of offenders revoked x 100.

Example: During 1994 there were 456 revocations. Of these, 310 were due to technical violations.

(310 ÷ 456) x 100 = 68%. **Objective was not achieved.**

and the overall rate of offender employment. A low rate of offender employment should suggest the development of job readiness and job placement services.

As in the case of drug/alcohol use, employment outcomes should also be examined within the context of recidivism rates. Do offenders who show improvements in employment have lower rates of recidivism? If so, employment programming should receive high priority within the agency.

Percentage of Revocations Due to Technical Violations. This outcome measure is a source of controversy. Some practitioners see a revocation, for any reason, as an indication of program failure. However, many practitioners argue that removing offenders from the streets because of technical violations pre-empts criminal behavior and, therefore, increases public safety (Wagner, 1989; Nidorf, 1991). These practitioners view an outcome measure such as the one provided in the example as an indicator of success rather

than failure. Regardless of the view adopted, such an outcome measure could only be viewed as a success if the overall rate of revocation was low.

Such controversy reinforces the need for process measures to determine what and how things are being done. For example, Anytown, USA has established a policy regarding the use of revocation in response to technical violations as a last resort to be used only after all other options have been tried or explored. In this case, a high number of revocations due to technical violations would cause administrators to question officers' practices. If after examining these practices, however, an administrator determines that officers are problem-solving with offenders, addressing needs, trying alternative methods to achieve case objectives and applying intermediate sanctions in response to noncompliance, then a high percentage of revocations due to technical violations rather than new arrests may be appropriate and desired. This scenario reiterates the importance of examining or developing agency values, mission and goals when establishing process and outcome measures.

Conclusion

There are numerous factors that contribute to a community's crime rate. The job of probation and parole agencies is to minimize the risk posed by offenders under community supervision. Thorough assessment and comprehensive case planning assists officers in identifying offenders' risks and needs, controlling offenders' risks, addressing offenders' criminogenic needs, and ultimately reducing their likelihood of reoffending. Intervention, surveillance, and enforcement strategies provide the opportunity for long-term behavioral change and short-term risk control, both of which are essential to community protection.

There are many ways in which a community corrections agency can document its efforts to protect the community and measure its achievements. Each of the measures discussed provide important information about the effectiveness of various probation and parole activities. None of them, however, can be viewed in isolation. They must all be considered in conjunction with the bottom line -- recidivism. The importance of documenting outcomes such as progress in treatment or employment, in addition to recidivism, is predicated on empirical evidence and theoretical arguments that they are linked to reduced recidivism.

The next chapter expands on the assessment and case planning required to assist offenders to change. As indicated previously, studies have shown that effective intervention and services can reduce recidivism. By tracking intervention outcomes and linking them with recidivism, agencies can begin to determine which of their programs and activities seem to most effectively protect the community.

CHAPTER SIX

ASSIST OFFENDERS TO CHANGE

GOAL: The Anytown, USA Community Corrections Department will assist offenders to change through the use of thorough assessments of needs and appropriate interventions.

Introduction

As discussed in previous chapters, recidivism among offenders in America's criminal justice system is a critical problem. Chapter Five, *Protect the Community*, outlined key correctional strategies (i.e., retribution, deterrence, incapacitation, and rehabilitation) and specific probation and parole activities designed to reduce an offender's likelihood of reoffending. This chapter will focus on rehabilitative strategies and interventions designed to assist offenders to change. Indeed, without interventions to assist offenders in changing their behaviors and thought processes, time spent in corrections programs is likely only to hold illicit behaviors in check for a brief period, and recidivism will remain a prominent concern.

While many offenders may genuinely profess a desire to change, without help in altering behaviors, learning new skills, and formulating different attitudes, they are unlikely to be successful in accomplishing the changes needed. Thus, it must be part of the mission of community corrections agencies to assist offenders to change. This requires officers to play a carefully balanced role which includes providing services, modeling prosocial behaviors, problem-solving, *and* taking a firm, fair approach to noncompliance. This chapter will examine several impor

tant steps in the behavioral change process including offender assessments, intervention planning, provision of services, and monitoring techniques. Examples of measurements for evaluating an agency's performance in this critical goal area also will be provided.

Rationale for Goal

In developing program mission statements, as well as objectives for individual case planning, it is important to consider the goals of intervention. For many years there has been a chasm between the goals of correctional programs and those of various social and mental health treatment approaches. On the one hand, the criminal justice system has been charged with the responsibility of imposing "just deserts" and exacting a degree of retribution on offenders. On the other hand, social and mental health services often have approached intervention in terms of compensation for deficits in earlier life experiences, rehabilitation, and restoration of the individual to productive living, sometimes to the exclusion of holding persons accountable for their offenses.

Current thinking about the function of correctional programs requires a much more holistic approach -- one that looks at the needs of the whole person and considers his or her develop mental history, current environment, behavior, and strengths and weaknesses. Maloney, Romig & Armstrong (1988) have developed a Balanced Approach for juvenile justice which is equally applicable to the entire criminal justice system. This approach posits that the justice system has three equally important responsibilities. These are:

- **Community protection**. As suggested in the previous chapter, ensuring the safety of all citizens is an important responsibility of government. When necessary, this means protecting vulnerable citizens from those who victimize them through various illegal activities. The criminal justice system has the responsibility of apprehending and adjudicating persons accused of illegal activities. If they are found guilty, offenders are to be supervised by correctional programs, either while incarcerated or in the community, as a means of preventing further offenses and harm to other citizens.

- **Offender accountability**. Historically, holding offenders accountable for their crimes has been a primary focus of the criminal justice system. Capital punishment and incarceration were the most common means of making offenders pay for their crimes. The cost to the offender was either their lives or their freedom. Over time, additional means of accountability have developed, including supervision in the community which often includes a partial loss of freedom through various supervision and surveillance techniques, fines, restitution, and community service.

- **Competency development**. This aspect of the Balanced Approach makes it different from earlier models of criminal justice. Many offenders have experienced deficits in their personal and social development. These may be manifested in dynamic attributes of

offenders and their circumstances that can change over time, such as attitudes toward employment, peers, authority, and substance abuse (Gendreau, Cullen, & Bonta, 1994). To help offenders change from a criminal lifestyle to one that is socially acceptable and productive, such areas must be assessed and addressed. Competency development, as a part of the mission of community corrections programs, calls for interventions that help offenders learn needed skills and develop prosocial attitudes and behaviors.

It is this latter responsibility of the criminal justice system that will be the topic of discussion for this chapter. Throughout the chapter, the case example of Robert Davis will be used to illustrate the principles and recommendations for assessment and intervention aimed at assisting offenders to change.

Probation and Parole Activities

Assessment of Offenders[1]

A major aspect of the Balanced Approach (Maloney, Romig & Armstrong, 1988) requires an *individualized assessment* of each offender. It is important to view each person as a whole and unique entity having a particular set of strengths and problems. Such an appraisal assists in formulating the most appropriate intervention plans and determining the level of risk to the offender and the community. Assessment, as discussed here, however, goes beyond risk/need assessment as described in the previous chapter.

A "one size fits all" approach to intervening with offenders is not successful. Palmer (1984) states that offenders differ from each other in terms of the primary causes of illegal behavior, their present situation, and future prospects. These particular characteristics of offenders help channel them to the most effective intervention options. Assessments that help sort out the level of risk presented and offenders' specific needs can be used to steer them to appropriate interventions based on principal tasks they need to complete, areas of focus for the intervention, and particular approaches which are most appropriate for their needs (Gendreau, Cullen & Bonta, 1994; Palmer, 1984).

Assessment implies an extensive undertaking to determine the severity of an offender's problems, evaluate contributing co-factors, and examine personal and social resources. From this process, recommendations for interventions are generated. Without a thorough assessment, intervening with offenders is similar to starting a trip without a map. Both the final destination (or treatment goal), and the means for reaching it, may remain elusive.

Assessment is not limited to a specific point in the community corrections process. It should occur continually from the point of entry in the system until release. Information acquired through assessments, and resulting recommendations, should follow each offender's journey through the criminal justice system. There are three key elements of the assessment process: gathering information; evaluating data; and making decisions.

Gathering Information. As suggested in Chapter Three, PSI's provide a good basis of information regarding offenders' past and present situations and current needs. However, a more comprehensive examination of this information may be required to develop appropriate intervention plans designed to assist offenders to change.

Assessment is a multi-faceted process, and a variety of techniques should be used to achieve the best results. For discussion, the information gathering process can be divided into three components:

1) investigation of existing information;
2) offender and collateral interviews; and
3) testing instruments.

To develop an appropriate intervention plan, background information about offenders can be vital. There are several resources through which background information about criminal justice offenders can be acquired. These may include existing criminal justice system records, school and employment records, and medical and mental health treatment records. The reason for requesting such information should be clearly related to the offender's current situation, and unrelated material should remain confidential.

Interviews with offenders, used in conjunction with other data collected in the assessment process, can provide a comprehensive picture of the offender's current status and needs. A good offender assessment interview also may be the foundation for a positive working relationship with the offender.

Through collateral interviews, pertinent information may be gathered from other persons who are or have been associated with the offender, such as family members, peers, teachers, and employers. Collateral sources should be asked to provide factual, descriptive information rather than to form judgments about the offender.

Various testing instruments can be helpful in assessing offenders regarding particular areas of functioning (e.g., personality, aggressive tendencies, social skills, stress factors, risk for substance abuse, intellectual capacity). Some of these must be used by professionals who are particularly trained in their use, while others are designed to be used by persons with minimal training in using the particular tool.

There are three general categories of testing instruments:

- *Standardized interviews* limit the interviewer to a prescribed style and list of questions. The interviewer does not have latitude to freely probe beyond conflicting or superficial answers to questions by the interviewee. Administration of these interviews usually requires minimal training; however, the interpretation of results may call for more extensive training. As standardized interviews are consistently administered and scored, validity and reliability studies may be available.

- *Structured interviews* are designed to obtain as much information as possible about the offender. Therefore, the interviewer is *expected* to probe beyond superficial or conflicting answers. Structured interviews require the person administering them to be proficient in conducting interviews. In addition, knowledge and experience working with the offender population are required. Structured interviews usually take more time to administer and interpret than standardized interviews.

- *Self-administered tests* can be helpful for those who have difficulty speaking directly about themselves. They provide an indirect, less threatening method of self-disclosing information. They also eliminate the possibility of interviewer bias and, like other standardized instruments, they can be scored and quantified. They usually have been investigated for reliability and validity. Such tests usually require less staff skill and training to administer. However, tests require some degree of motivation and reading ability on the part of the offender being assessed. Of course, self-administered tests are only credible if the offender is willing to answer the questions honestly.

Testing instruments are a *tool* to guide decisionmaking efforts. As with all other techniques, the limitations of tests must be realized. Staff members with responsibility for administering and interpreting tests should be fully trained.

Evaluation of Assessment Data. After information is gathered, it must be interpreted for use in decisionmaking. During this phase, professional service providers (e.g., probation/parole officers, addiction counselors, group therapists, psychiatrists) attempt to determine the severity of the offender's problems, possible contributing factors, and the offender's readiness for intervention. Personal characteristics of the offender which may influence treatment outcomes should be considered such as conceptual level, cognitive functioning, psychiatric history, and motivation. Mitigating social factors should also considered. The financial, social, and employment resources of offenders and their families may influence the intervention plan. For example, if a drug-involved offender is economically disadvantaged and the only community drug treatment resources available are financed by private insurance payments, the offender will not be eligible.

In addition to the information gathered during the PSI (Figure 27), Robert was referred to the Mental Health Center for additional assessment. Figure 50 lists the assessment procedures administered and provides a summary of the findings.

Decisionmaking. After the assessment data has been evaluated, the process of addressing the rehabilitative needs of the offender begins. Case management decisions and recommendations for interventions are developed and implemented. In addition to offender-specific information, available agency resources must also be examined. The size of caseloads, number of personnel, staff interests and abilities, special programs, legal requirements, and many other factors define services that can be provided within the agency. Community services play a

Figure 50 - Assessment Report: Robert J. Davis

SUMMARY OF THE ASSESSMENT REPORT FOR ROBERT DAVIS

Date of interview with offender: January 10, 1994

Summary of interview: During the initial stages of the interview Robert appeared somewhat nervous and hesitant to provide too much information. Once the purpose of the interview was explained (i.e., to develop a plan to assist him with some of the problems he was encountering) he opened up a bit and was generally cooperative and congenial. Robert indicated that he drinks on a daily basis but that he did not feel that his drinking caused him any problems. When questioned about his problems with employment and the domestic violence charge he became defensive and blamed his employers and his wife for "messing with him for no reason." Robert would not engage in a discussion about his childhood or family. His affect was generally flat when questioned about his relationship with his parents and his father's death. When asked about his plans for the future, he indicated that he "just wants to get this court stuff over with" and that he would like to get a job and move out of his mother's home.

Tests Administered:

Weschler Adult Intelligence Scale - Revised (WAIS-R)
Minnesota Multiphasic Personality Inventory (MMPI)
Substance Abuse Assessment Instrument (SAAI)

Summary of assessment tests: The results of the MMPI indicate characteristics of impulsiveness, high activity, a tendency to over-react to situations, alcoholism, and problems in developing and maintaining relationships.

The SAAI report stated that Robert has developed a dependency on alcohol and is prone to using other chemical substances to enhance or counteract the effects of alcohol.

On the WAIS-R, Robert scored in the low-normal range of intelligence with an overall score of 90. However, there was a considerable discrepancy between his verbal and performance scores indicating he may have a learning disability and is likely to experience difficulties in reading and language.

Mitigating social factors: Robert is currently unemployed and living with his mother. He has no financial means to pay for treatment.

Recommendations: Robert rationalizes his behavior and, while fairly cooperative, seems unmotivated to change at this time. He will require a highly structured program; the legal leverage of the court may motivate him to, at least, attend the recommended treatment programs. Robert's assessment indicates that he requires intensive alcohol treatment. His previous failure with outpatient treatment suggests that inpatient treatment may be more appropriate, however, it is recommended that an intensive outpatient program with drug testing and strict enforcement strategies be attempted initially. It is also recommended that Robert be required to participate in a Batterer's Group to address his issues of domestic violence.

---

vital part in accomplishing a community corrections agency's mission and the individual case intervention goals for each offender. Formal community resources include services such as drug treatment programs, educational programs, health care, social welfare systems, and religious organizations. Employment opportunities, recreation programs, and social clubs are also important community resources. The combination of supervision, treatment strategies, and resources selected to intervene with a given offender will be largely subjective. Because each offender is different, varied interventions should be outlined in individual plans as described below.

Intervention Planning

The case planning process outlined in Chapter Five involved identifying and prioritizing risks and needs, establishing behavioral objectives, and specifying resources for meeting those objectives. This section will expand upon that case planning process to include detailed intervention planning designed to address offenders' deficiencies and assist them to change. These detailed intervention plans may be developed by probation and parole officers or by treatment providers. They are instructional within this context in that they clearly outline specific offender objectives, the role of probation and parole officers and/or other service providers, and outcome measures for assessing individual offender progress.

There are two important parts of intervention planning: 1) establishing goals for intervention; and 2) matching the needs of offenders with appropriate interventions.

Goals and Objectives for Intervening with Offenders. Treatment goals and objectives should state what the offender will be able to do, or what changes will be made as a result of the intervention. Goals are general statements of what should be accomplished. Objectives are steps required to achieve a goal. They should be specific to the offender's identified needs and problems, and they should be measurable and time-limited. They should include the following elements:

• What action is to be taken. They should describe exactly what the offender must do to meet the objective.

• Criteria for successful completion. This is the measurement to be used (e.g., three months of negative urinalyses; sixty hours of community service) to determine that the offender has accomplished a particular objective.

• Time frame. This refers to the length of the intervention and/or when it will begin and end. The time frame may be fixed or it may depend on successful completion of certain tasks by the offender.

• Persons responsible. The offender, as well as other persons, such as the probation/parole officer or other service providers, may be accountable for each task.

• Expected benefits and consequences. The offender should understand and anticipate positive results and rewards if the intervention objectives are completed. In the sample intervention plan (Figure 51), urinalysis would be discontinued when the offender has three months of negative tests. The offender should also be clear about sanctions that will be imposed in response to noncompliance with the intervention plan. The sample plan includes verbal reprimands, earlier curfews or house arrest and residential placement as possible sanctions for a positive test.

Figure 51 provides a sample intervention plan containing these elements that was prepared for Robert Davis.

Offender-Treatment Matching. The assessment process will reveal a constellation of problems, needs and resources that is unique to each offender. Thus, intervention plans must be fashioned individually to address this distinctive configuration. There are at least three important reasons effective offender-treatment matching is essential.

- **Improved success**. When individuals receive the intervention that is most appropriate for their needs, they are more likely to respond positively and continue with the intervention until treatment goals have been accomplished.

- **Programmatic efficiency**. No program is designed to meet the needs of every individual. Offender-treatment matching helps channel persons with specific problems or needs to the most appropriate programs for them. This results in more effective use of scarce resources. If offenders are not matched with the appropriate intervention program for their assessed needs, the programmatic resource will be misused, and other persons who might benefit from that particular intervention may be excluded from entering the program because of limited program space.

- **Financial savings**. When individuals receive appropriate treatment, money is saved. If interventions are suitable for an individual's needs, the offender is much more likely to benefit from them. However, if an intervention is inappropriate, the offender is not likely to benefit from it and the money for it will be spent unwisely.

Offender-treatment matching is not an exact science. It often is necessary to adjust case plans following periodic reassessment of an individual's progress. Intervention may include both *traditional community corrections approaches* such as supervision, drug testing, electronic monitoring, fines, restitution and community service; and services that typically have been classified as *treatment*, such as individual and group counseling, skill development, and other therapeutic interventions.

Andrews, Bonta, and Hoge (1990) have identified the following four principles that should be considered in selecting appropriate service options for offenders:

- **Risk**. Higher risk offenders require higher levels of services. Higher risk offenders respond better to intensive services, while lower risk offenders usually do as well or better with less intensive services.

- **Need**. Services should be matched to the needs of offenders that are amenable to change (e.g., drug abuse, home/school/job problems, antisocial attitudes, and associations). Changes in these areas frequently result in reductions in recidivism.

- **Responsivity**. This refers to offender characteristics such as learning styles and abilities that can be matched with styles and modes of service provision.

- **Professional judgment**. While risk, need and responsivity should be considered, assessments of these areas are not perfect. Professional experience and judgment are always factors in matching offenders with appropriate services.

Implementation of the Intervention Plan

There are three basic types of services that may need to be provided to offenders: *correctional services, treatment services*, and *basic living services*. Many of these may be provided within

Figure 51 - Intervention Plan: Robert J. Davis

INTERVENTION PLAN

Name: Robert J. Davis (W/M)   Age: 22   DOB: 4/14/70

Address: 325 W. Maple Avenue, Springfield 50532

Goal 1:   **Robert will function appropriately in society without using drugs and alcohol.**

Objective a.   Robert will undergo random urinalysis each week at the Probation Department until he has tested negative for drug use for three consecutive months.

Intervention Plan: Robert will be entered in the drug testing program. He will attend an orientation session to explain the rules. He will be assigned a color code and will be required to call in daily to find out if he is to report for testing each day. He will be required to give a urine specimen each week which will be tested in-house. The results will be recorded in his case record. For negative test results, Robert will be given positive feedback from the probation officer. For each full month that he has all negative tests, a letter of commendation will be sent to the Judge with a copy given to Robert. For each positive urinalysis, Robert will be sanctioned. Possible sanctions include verbal reprimands, earlier curfews, house arrest and residential placement. If Robert receives four positive test results in a row, the court will be notified that he is not complying with the conditions of his probation.

Outcome Measures: A log will be maintained to track the results of Robert's urinalyses. Measures of success will include increasing intervals of time between positive test results. When Robert receives three straight months of negative results, drug testing will be considered successful, and he will be required to provide a specimen only if the probation officer suspects current drug use.

Objective b: Robert will participate in outpatient treatment for alcoholism at the Mental Health Center.

Intervention Plan: Robert will be referred to the alcoholism treatment program and will be required to attend individual and group counseling sessions. He also will be required to attend two AA meetings per week. His counselor at the Mental Health Center will determine the length of time Robert needs to remain in treatment. Any failure to attend treatment or AA will result in sanctions. Regular attendance will be noted in Robert's case record and reported to the court at appropriate intervals.

Outcome Measures: Robert's attendance at the treatment program and AA meetings will be closely monitored through weekly checks with his counselor and his AA sponsor. Robert is expected to attend all meetings unless he has a doctor's

---

excuse. There will be a monthly contact with his counselor to determine Robert's level of participation and cooperation in the treatment program. His progress toward maintaining sobriety will be evaluated with his counselor at three month intervals.

Goal 2:   **Robert will participate in treatment for domestic violence.**

Objective a: Robert will be referred to the Batterer's Treatment Program run by Safe Place, Inc.

Intervention Plan: Robert will attend weekly group treatment meetings for 26 weeks. He will be instructed to participate and cooperate in the sessions. Failure to attend meetings will result in sanctions. Regular attendance and cooperation will be noted in his case record and reported to the Judge.

Outcome Measures: Weekly checks of Robert's attendance will be made. Monthly contacts with the program coordinator will determine Robert's level of participation and cooperation. Every three months, the program coordinator will submit a written report concerning Robert's progress in the group.

Objective b: Robert will abide by the conditions of the Emergency Protective Order (EPO) and have no contact with his wife and daughter.

Intervention Plan: Robert will be instructed that disregarding the EPO will result in the probation officer filing contempt of court charges. The Officer will tell Diane Davis to notify him if Robert disregards the order. She also will be offered the services of a Victim Advocate to help her develop a safety plan and obtain any other services she needs for herself or her child. Initially, the Probation Officer will phone Diane Davis weekly to inquire as to whether there are problems with Robert obeying the EPO. Contacts will be decreased if Robert complies with the EPO.

Outcome Measures: Any instances during which Robert is out of compliance with the EPO will be noted and will result in contempt of court charges. However, the absence of violations noted in the case file throughout Robert's period of probation, or until the EPO is rescinded, will indicate successful completion of this objective.

Goal 3:   **Robert will be evaluated concerning his educational and vocational training needs and he will receive the services needed to prepare him for productive employment.**

Objective a: Within two weeks, Robert will be referred to Vocational Rehabilitation for an assessment of his educational and vocational training needs.

Intervention Plan:	A referral for assessment will be made. Robert will be instructed to attend the evaluation sessions and cooperate with the assessment process. Failure to attend or cooperate will result in sanctions.
Outcome Measures:	A detailed assessment of Robert's educational and vocational training needs will indicate successful completion of this objective.
Objective b:	If deemed appropriate by the assessment, Robert will be referred to the Adult Education Program for help in obtaining his GED.
Intervention Plan:	Unless the Assessment indicates it would be counterproductive, Robert will be required to spend at least 8 hours per week at the Adult Education Program working toward obtaining his GED. Weekly attendance checks will be made, and monthly progress reports will be requested. Failure to attend and participate will result in sanctions. A positive attendance record and progress will be noted and rewarded.
Outcome Measures:	Documentation of attendance and progress toward obtaining the GED will be used to indicate success for this objective. Ultimately obtaining the GED will be expected.
Objective c:	Based on the vocational assessment, Robert will be referred for training.
Intervention Plan:	Robert will be referred to the Vocational Training Program to receive job training appropriate to his interests and abilities. When he is accepted into a program, he will be expected to attend regularly and to make acceptable progress for a full term. Failure to attend or participate will result in sanctions. Positive patterns of attendance and progress in the program will be rewarded.
Outcome Measures:	Regular attendance will be documented through weekly checks with the program. Monthly progress reports will be requested. Completion of the program will indicate ultimate success.

community corrections agencies. However, it is likely that many offenders will need interventions that can be provided only by other social service agencies within the community. Thus, developing a working knowledge of community resources and relationships with those who provide them is important for community corrections personnel. A complete discussion on coordinating community services is provided in Chapter Eight.

Correctional Services. Correctional services typically consist of endeavors that are aimed at protecting the community and holding offenders accountable. These are usually the responsibility of the criminal justice system. The following types of correctional services are among those characteristic of community corrections programs.

Traditional supervision. Offenders are assigned a probation or parole officer to whom they must report on a regular basis. Traditional supervision places some limits on offenders (e.g., places they may not go, activities they may not participate in, people they may not associate with), but they are able to live in the community, be employed and maintain family relationships.

Intensive supervision. More vigorous community supervision may be provided those who present a greater level of risk to public safety or are more likely to re-offend. This may include more frequent interactions with supervising officers and more exacting requirements for behaviors and participation in treatment.

Specialized caseloads. Some community corrections programs have organized specialized caseloads for groups of offenders having similar needs. For example, specialized caseloads may be comprised of drug-involved offenders, sex offenders, domestic violence offenders, or other specific groups. Often, particular programs, such as educational or treatment groups are provided for persons on specialized caseloads.

There are many program elements that may be included in any of the above forms of supervision and surveillance. Some of these are:

- electronic monitoring;
- drug testing;
- home detention and curfews; and
- day reporting centers.

In addition to supervision, other conditions that hold them accountable may be imposed on offenders, such as community service and financial sanctions. *Community service* can develop skills, enhance the self-esteem of offenders, and provide needed services to other citizens. However, in considering the assignment of offenders to community service activities, their propensity for criminal activities must be low enough that they will not pose a danger to other

citizens by their relative freedom in the community (Singer, 1992).

Financial restitution may be ordered to repay the victim for property damages, medical expenses, lost wages, counseling and other costs resulting from the offense. *Fines*, on the other hand, may be levied to require offenders to pay a debt to society. Fines usually are scaled according to the severity of the crime, and sometimes the ability of the offender to pay. *User fees* may be charged for probation supervision and services. The money charged helps offenders realize the value of services they receive and helps counter the rising cost of the criminal justice system.

Treatment Services. Treatment services for offenders will vary according to the needs of the offenders and the individualized case plans developed for them. Treatment services may be offered within the community corrections agency or by other community agencies. Although they will vary in content, treatment services often include one or more of the following approaches:

- individual counseling or therapy;
- family counseling or therapy;
- group counseling or therapy;
- educational interventions and skill development;
- self-help and support groups; and
- medical treatment.

Basic Living Services. Offenders, like everyone else, must have certain fundamental goods and services. Without these, they are less likely to be able to maintain a prosocial lifestyle. These include but are not limited to:

- affordable housing that meets at least minimum standards;
- food;
- clothing; and

- income, which may require job skills and employment services.

Making Referrals

As just mentioned, not all services needed by offenders will be available within community corrections agencies. When referrals are necessary, community corrections professionals need appropriate skills and information. Maintaining a working list or directory of community agencies and resources
is important, and it should be updated periodically.

As already mentioned, matching offender needs and treatment services is cost effective, programmatically efficient, and likely to result in better treatment outcomes. Appropriate referrals also require effective referral processes and mechanisms. These may range from simple methods of having offenders or officers call the agency to more elaborate referral forms that must be completed. It is important to provide adequate information when making a referral. This may include details about the offender and should always include the specific problem(s) to be addressed or the particular service(s) needed. Many interagency relations have been strained because referrals were not precise enough and the receiving agency, therefore, did not provide the appropriate service.

Of course, confidentiality of offender information is important. Only the information needed for another agency to determine offender eligibility or provide effective services should be shared. For certain types of services, such as drug and alcohol treatment, there are strict federal, and sometimes state, laws that protect offender confidentiality. Community corrections professionals must be aware of, and carefully abide by, such regulations.

Monitoring Service Provision and Offender Compliance

Gendreau and Andrews (1990) have identified the firm and fair enforcement of program contingencies (e.g., attending program sessions, abstaining from alcohol use) as a key principle of effective intervention. This enforcement requires careful monitoring of service provision and offender compliance. If offenders are unable to perform certain tasks or access certain resources, the plan may need to be altered. However, if offenders are unwilling to carry out their responsibilities, treatment programs or community corrections programs should impose an appropriate sanction. Community corrections agencies have the power of the court or parole board to enforce compliance.

Accurate documentation of offender performance is an essential element of service monitoring. Community corrections professionals should keep records of attendance and participation at individual and group meetings within the agency, as well as those services to which the offender is referred outside the community corrections agency. Ongoing communication between community corrections and other service providers is vital so there will not be lapses between an offenders' failure to attend and some type of sanctioning by community corrections. Not only should problems be documented, but progress and positive responses by offenders also should be recorded. This information is especially helpful in making fair decisions if a offender encounters problems.

If offenders do not comply with the requirements of their case plan, the causes must be assessed. Sometimes noncompliance is a choice; other times it is a result of circumstances that cannot be controlled. Confrontation and enforcement should be based on this assessment. Motivating offenders to comply with case plans may include rewards for compliance or sanctions for noncompliance (National Center for Juvenile Justice, 1991). Sanctions might include increased supervision, additional loss of freedoms, or return to court. Sanctions should progress gradually from least to most restrictive. Robert's intervention plan (Figure 51) includes rewards for progress and sanctions for noncompliance.

It is also possible that an agency or professional outside of community corrections may shirk their responsibilities or fail to comply with the case plan. If this occurs, ultimate sanctions might include censure or withdrawal of offenders, but less drastic means of encouraging improved performance should be attempted initially.

Aftercare

Some offenders will need ongoing services after they complete certain treatment programs. This is especially important with substance abuse, domestic violence, and sexual offenses. Periodic checks should be made with offenders and collateral contacts. If the offender continues to be under the supervision of a community corrections agency, this is relatively easy. If, however, the offender is no longer on probation or parole, it still may be important for someone to have occasional contact. Sometimes treatment agencies can provide this service. Just providing encouragement and maintaining interest in offenders can be helpful to their continued progress and prosocial behavior.

Evaluation

A final and vitally important step in case planning and intervention is evaluation. On an individual and collective basis, community corrections agencies and professionals should continually evaluate the effectiveness of interventions. This is the only rational way to make effective decisions about programs and about offenders. Evaluation includes measures of the

process and the outcomes of service provision. Individual outcome measures for Robert are included in the intervention plan. The final section of this chapter examines some of the alternative measures for assessing offender and program outcomes.

Performance-Based Measures

There are a variety of data that can be gathered to assess the effectiveness of interventions. The most commonly used measure has been recidivism rates. However, this may or may not be an accurate indicator of progress made by offenders. The Intervention Plan shows measures that can be used for individual offenders. This section will address similar measures in an aggregated format for agency wide evaluation. The following are areas for which factual information can be obtained and documented to determine if treatment and services are being delivered as designed and if they are assisting offenders to change.

Process Measures

Attendance. Attendance and/or participation in treatment and supervision programs usually can be easily documented. A pattern of good attendance often suggests cooperation and progress that may be noted in other areas, as well. On the other hand, poor attendance may be correlated with negative results on other measures. The point is, that intervention outcomes are only meaningful once it has been determined that offenders are, in fact, attending the program.

Possible reasons for low attendance rates should be examined. They could be due to individual problems experienced by offenders such as transportation problems or basic refusal to attend. In the first case, methods for facilitating transportation could be explored. In the second case, sanctions for noncompliance with treatment

Figure 52 - Rates of Attendance in Outpatient Treatment

Objective: Overall attendance rates for offenders participating in the community outpatient treatment program will be no less than 75% during the first quarter of 1994.

Data elements: Total number of sessions required for all offenders, total number of sessions attended for all offenders.

Formula: Total number of sessions attended ÷ total number of sessions required x 100.

Example: 160 offenders were referred to the community outpatient treatment program. Each offender was required to attend 12 sessions during the first quarter of 1994 for a total of 1920 required sessions. The cumulative number of sessions attended was 1133.

(1133 ÷ 1920) x 100 = 59%. **Objective was not achieved.**

orders should be clearly outlined for the offender and imposed where necessary. Another contributing factor may be a lack of communication between treatment personnel and probation/parole officers. Community corrections can provide the legal leverage required by some offenders to attend treatment. However, if officers are unaware of attendance problems they cannot take corrective action.

Degree of Implementation of the Intervention Plan. Intervention planning is just one step in the behavioral change process. Agencies may choose to establish a performance measure for determining the extent to which the plans are being carried out. Case chronologies and progress reports of randomly selected cases could be reviewed to determine if the actions taken reflect

the intervention goals and objectives. Each case could then be rated as "fully implemented, partially implemented, or not implemented." Reasons for a low degree of implementation should be explored. Supervisors could then use this information to make recommendations to officers for improving intervention planning and implementation. Until the degree of implementation is ascertained, outcomes of the intervention plan provide limited information for policy decisions.

Figure 53 - Degree of Implementation

Objective: 80% of the case files reviewed for intervention planning and implementation will be rated as "fully implemented."

Data elements: Number of cases reviewed, number of cases rated as fully implemented.

Formula: Number of cases rated as fully implemented ÷ number of cases reviewed x 100.

Example: 80 case files were reviewed. 52 of these case files were rated as "fully implemented."

(52 ÷ 80) x 100 = 65% **Objective was not achieved.**

Outcome Measures

Cooperation and Attitude. Antisocial attitudes (e.g., toward authority, education and employment; aggression; impulsivity) are strong predictors of recidivism (Gendreau, 1994). Therefore, it would be important to have information regarding the extent to which a specific intervention changes these attitudes. These characteristics often are more difficult to document objectively. However, through careful observations by all persons involved with the offender (e.g., community corrections and

Figure 54 - Percent of Offenders Showing Improvement in Attitude

Objective: 70% of offenders completing the domestic violence treatment group will show an improvement in attitude as demonstrated by pre- and post-measures.

Data elements: Number of offenders completing the treatment program, number of offenders showing progress in program.

Formula: Number of offenders showing improvement $\div$ number of offenders completing the program x 100.

Example: 87 offenders participated in the domestic violence treatment group. 43 of them showed improvements in attitudes as demonstrated by pre- and post-measures.

$(43 \div 87) \times 100 = 49\%$ **Objective was not achieved.**

treatment professionals, collateral contacts), changes over time can be noted. In some cases, it may even be desirable to have offenders respond to simple Likert-type scales that provide a pre- and post-intervention measure of attitudes.

Research findings suggest that reassessments on criminogenic needs, such as antisocial attitudes, improves the ability to predict recidivism (Andrews, 1989) and can, therefore, lead to improved service delivery and resource allocation. Because of the strong correlation between antisocial attitudes and criminal behavior, targeting attitudes is a promising means of reducing recidivism. Improvements in attitude should be examined in conjunction with recidivism rates to determine if, in fact, recidivism rates decreased. Information of this nature confirms the importance of providing treatment and services aimed at assisting the offender to change.

The low rate of offender improvement in the example provided suggests that the treatment program be assessed for effectiveness. Among key questions to explore are: What modality of treatment is being used? What levels and types of expertise do the treatment providers possess? And are offenders referred to the treatment program appropriate for participation? Answers to these and other critical questions may provide insight to these low improvement rates.

<u>Progress in Supervision and Treatment</u>. Depending on the assessed needs of offenders and the type of interventions provided, measurements of progress can be made by pre- and post-intervention comparisons. For example, for drug- or alcohol-involved offenders, the number of days during which they remain free of drugs or alcohol (as documented through urinalysis) and/or increasing intervals of time between

Figure 55 - Number of Days Drug Free

Objective: 85% of the offenders successfully completing the Inpatient Treatment Program during FY 1994 will remain drug free for a period of 90 days from the date of release as documented by urinalysis.

Data Elements: Number of offenders successfully completing the program, number of offenders who remained drug free.

Formula: Number of offenders who remained drug free $\div$ number of offenders successfully completing program x 100.

Example: 112 offenders successfully completed the program. 84 of these offenders remained drug free for a minimum period of 90 days.

$(84 \div 112) \times 100 = 75\%$ **Objective was not achieved.**

positive urinalyses can be indicators of progress. A high frequency of testing (i.e., a minimum of two tests per week) would be needed to make this outcome a valid measure of progress.

Progress for offenders who are participating in various types of education, treatment or counseling can be judged through reports of attendance, grades and/or progress reports from the professionals involved. For offenders needing assistance with job training and employment, attendance, performance, and length of employment are easily documented measures of progress.

Interpersonal Functioning and Responsibilities. While this is also a somewhat subjective area of evaluation, it is one that should be included. Interactions with family, friends, co-workers and employers often substantiate improvements in offender attitudes and performance. It would, however, be advisable to obtain data from multiple sources to validate reports from close associates. Family responsibilities might include some areas that can be quantified, as well, such as the payment of child support. Work or professional functioning may include attendance and work performance. In many cases improvements in these areas are easily quantifiable.

Data such as that provided in the example could be used as one indicator of the effectiveness of various treatment groups or services. In this case, participants in an anger control group are reassessed every three months to determine how effectively they are coping with anger. Self-administered pre- and post-tests are completed by the participants to measure improvements. A structured interview format is then used to obtain consistent information from family members, employers and treatment providers to corroborate this information. An overall rating is then assigned to the offender to indicate the level of improvement or a lack of improvement.

Figure 56 - Level of Improvement in Controlling Anger

Objective: A three month reassessment of participants in Anger Control Groups during FY 1994 will reveal a minimum improvement of two rankings for 70% of the participants.

Data elements: Number of offenders participating in anger control groups, initial rankings, rankings at three month reassessment, number of offenders improving by two rankings at three month assessment.

Formula: Number of offenders improving by two rankings at three month assessment ÷ number of offenders participating in anger control group x 100.

Example: 96 offenders participated in Anger Control Groups during FY 1994. 72 of the participants showed improvements in their ability to control anger by two rankings as measured by three month reassessments of each participant.

(72 ÷ 96) x 100 = 75%. **Objective was achieved.**

Assessment processes similar to the one proposed in this scenario are particularly important during the beginning stages of a new service or program. They can be conducted by the treatment providers or by community corrections personnel. Many agencies require services with whom they contract to include some type of evaluative component that measures offender improvement. The data can then be used to guide program improvements.

Conclusion

This chapter has discussed the vital role of intervening with offenders in community corrections programs as a means to promoting behavioral change. Effective interventions require a thorough, individualized assessment process which becomes the basis for intervention planning. Assisting offenders to change requires interventions that address offenders' needs and hold them accountable for their own progress and behaviors.

Measuring the success of interventions and, specifically, the extent to which they promote behavioral change is essential. By monitoring individual progress and outcomes, officers and offenders can modify intervention plans as needed to achieve case objectives. Individual case outcomes can then be aggregated to assess the overall effectiveness of various intervention techniques and programs. Performance-based measures such as program attendance and improvements in interpersonal functioning provide valuable information upon which to base program modifications and improvements, and ultimately will impact an agency's ability to achieve other important organizational goals.

---

[1] Information in this section was adapted from the following sources:

American Probation and Parole Association & National Association of Probation Executives. (1988). *National Narcotics Intervention Training Program.*

Crowe, A. H., & Schaefer, P. J. (1992). *Identifying and Intervening with Drug-Involved Youth* (Chapter 11). Lexington, KY: American Probation and Parole Association.

CHAPTER SEVEN

SUPPORT CRIME VICTIMS

GOAL:	The Anytown, USA Community Corrections Department will support crime victims by remaining sensitive to their concerns and by addressing their needs and interests throughout the processing, supervision and termination of a case.

One of the most neglected subjects in the study of crime is its victims...
The President's Commission on Law Enforcement and the Administration of Justice, 1967

Introduction

The emphasis on victims' rights in the criminal justice system has increased significantly over the past few years due to the powerful voice of victim advocacy groups. Courts and parole boards are beginning to recognize the need to address victims' concerns in the sentencing and release processes. Prosecutors' offices often provide a comprehensive range of victim services. Still, community corrections practices are largely offender-directed and tend to ignore the concerns of crime victims. As seen in the preceding goal-specific chapters, supervision strategies are aimed at protecting the public as a whole from further victimization. Unfortunately, however, the interests of individual victims are often lost among the burgeoning caseloads of offenders and the accompanying paperwork.

This chapter offers several compelling reasons for probation and parole agencies to transform these *offender-directed* practices into those that are also *victim-centered*. More importantly, perhaps, it advocates for practices that are *principle-centered* and address issues common to all sides such as accountability, rationality, efficiency, and fairness. Assessing and addressing the informational needs and interests of

victims is a critical function of community corrections agencies. This chapter will discuss specific activities related to supporting the rights of victims and corresponding performance-based measures which demonstrate that services to victims and services to offenders do not have to be mutually exclusive.

Rationale for Goal

As public service agencies, and a key component of the criminal justice system, community corrections should concern themselves with justice for *all* citizens. While the primary avenue for achieving this justice may be through the provision of supervision and services to offenders, it does not have to be at the exclusion of serving others impacted by crime. Specifically, community corrections agencies can, and often do, provide valuable services to victims of crime.

Throughout the prosecutorial stage of the criminal justice system, victim services are generally provided by the prosecutor's office or victim-witness programs. Many victims, however, contend that the trial phase does not bring closure to the pain and suffering caused by the criminal. Loss of property and fear for personal safety are issues with which victims still must grapple. Furthermore, many victims suffer a "secondary victimization" resulting from their experience with the criminal justice system; this complex experience can be disconcerting as victims often feel as if their needs and concerns are left unheard and unaddressed (APPA, 1994b). Community corrections agencies can help victims cope with the pains of primary and secondary victimization by carefully assessing their needs and interests and providing them with information and services that address those needs and interests.

But why should this responsibility fall within the purview of community corrections? In addition to it being the "right thing to do" there are several practical reasons for making the provision of services to victims a priority. First, probation and parole have access to both general and offender-specific information that could address victims' informational needs and concerns. Just knowing how probation and parole work and that offenders will be held accountable for their actions (e.g., through the payment of restitution and other supervisory conditions) is often enough to ease the fears and frustrations of victims. Additionally, probation and parole professionals are familiar with the services available within the community to address offender needs. Victims have many of these same needs and could, therefore, benefit from this information.

Second, there is a continuing need for the profession to identify victims as consumers of probation and parole services. Many times victims are seen as being at odds with community corrections. Agencies such as South Carolina's Probation, Parole and Pardon Services have implemented comprehensive victim services and have come to recognize that victims groups can be powerful allies of community corrections if given the opportunity. Once invited into the folds of the system and educated on the mission of community corrections, victims groups have, in fact, provided support for probation and

parole services and spoken on their behalf in front of legislative bodies.

Third, victims groups can be effective in educating the general public about the mission of community corrections and, therefore, in enhancing their public image. The nature of the services provided by probation and parole, and the nature of the persons directly served are viewed negatively; probation and parole are not in the business of serving "deserved" constituents. This often alienates probation and parole agencies, keeping them literally estranged from the majority of people to whom they provide their service of ensuring public safety. The public typically hears about probation and parole only after an offender under their supervision commits a heinous crime. Providing victim services increases awareness of community corrections programs and demonstrates a true commitment to protecting public interests.

Fourth, in addition to being allies of community corrections at a policy level, victims may be helpful therapeutic agents in individual cases. Victim-offender mediation programs bring an offender and the victim together for a face-to-face meeting to discuss possible resolutions for victim losses such as a payment schedule for restitution, a letter of apology, or the performance of community service (Sinclair, 1994). Involvement in mediation programs may help both the victim and the probationer to realize things about each other that reduces their respective rationalizations (e.g., offenders' perception that "no-harm" was caused, and victims' misconceptions of offenders-as-demons).

Lastly, across the nation, many probation and parole agencies are being *required* to provide victim services because of legislative mandates. By this point, the manner in which these services are provided are not left to the discretion of these professional agencies, but are defined from the outside. This often leads to resentment and overburdened agencies. Community corrections agencies often cast themselves as victims of the system, at the mercy of judicial and parole board constraints, political powers, and legislative mandates. The constraints are very real. But it is the way that community corrections manages them that will determine their fate. The louder the voices of crime victims, the more these constraints will be felt, particularly in the form of legislative mandates. Instead of waiting for the hammer to fall, agencies can be proactive and develop victim services in a systematic and logical fashion, incorporating these extra duties in a manner that compliments, rather than complicates, existing services and responsibilities.

As can be seen, there are several compelling reasons for community corrections agencies to incorporate victim services into their mission and programs. The next section will discuss probation and parole activities that support the rights of crime victims and bring benefits to all those involved.

Probation and Parole Activities

Assessment of the Impact of the Crime upon the Victim

The Final Report of the President's Task Force on Crime published in 1982 included a key recommendation that "judges should allow for, and give appropriate weight to, input at sentencing from victims of violent crimes." Victim impact statements are a critical component of the process. A victim impact statement allows the victim to express how the criminal act has affected their life and allows the financial, emotional, physical, and psychological effects to be considered in the sentencing procedure.

The responsibility for issuing the victim impact statement and collecting the information frequently falls within the responsibilities of proba-

tion departments as part of the pre-sentence investigation activities. This information is then included in the pre-sentence investigation report. The extent to which probation agencies are involved with the victim at this stage is largely determined by departmental policies and the nature of the crime and varies from jurisdiction to jurisdiction. Some probation agencies determine the amount of restitution owed. Some agencies interview the victim to gather more detailed information regarding emotional or physical harm caused by the crime. At the parole stage, victim information is updated by institutional officers and presented to the parole board for consideration in the release decision. In any case, the complete and accurate assessment of victim losses is a critical activity performed by probation and parole agencies. The extent to which this is accomplished will impact the quality of services provided to victims.

Victim Notification

Victim notification, as a service within probation and parole, is much less prevalent than those services designed to assess the impact of crime. This service, however, is critically important to victims of crime. Victim notification refers to:

- advising the victim of the offender's custody status (e.g., is the offender incarcerated, being released on parole, in a residential setting);

- notifying victims of arrangements for the payment of restitution;

- informing victims of the offender's supervisory conditions; and

- notifying victims of potential danger.

The ongoing supervision and assessment of offenders and their established community-based network makes probation and parole agencies the logical unit of the criminal justice system to keep victims informed of the case status. This notification can occur in the form of telephone calls or letters. The confidential nature of probation and parole records and activities often causes a hesitancy to provide this information. Most of this information, however, is a matter of public record and can, therefore, be provided to victims without concern.

The specific informational interests of the victim should be carefully considered in the notification process. In some cases, such information can contribute to a victim's peace of mind; in others, victims may prefer not to be reminded of their experience. This sensitivity to the individual needs of crime victims demonstrates probation and parole's commitment to protecting their rights.

Managing Restitution Collection

The extent of officer involvement in the collection and disbursement of restitution depends upon local policies. In many jurisdictions officers are directly responsible for both of these activities and for establishing payment schedules with the offender. The most common role assumed by probation and parole, however, is to monitor restitution payments.

Just as with any other court/parole board-ordered condition of probation/parole, the officer is responsible for facilitating, monitoring and enforcing compliance with the payment of restitution. When the conditions have not been met, the officer should be responsible for notifying the appropriate individuals including the court, parole board, and victim. The collection of restitution is a tangible and common means for probation and parole agencies to support the rights of victims.

Referrals to Services

There are a number of services available to crime victims through the criminal justice system and through other community resources. To inform victims of these services, many agencies have developed one-page fact sheets, or brochures, which include the names, addresses and telephone numbers of various organizations and a brief description of the nature of their services. This is a fairly simple method for providing a valuable service to victims.

Education about Community Corrections

The criminal justice system is extremely complex. One of the best services probation and parole agencies can provide to victims is education about the system, and particularly about community corrections. A common request of victims is that they be educated about the operations of the community corrections agency, explanations of the rules by which offenders must abide, and guidance regarding who to contact for answers to victims' questions (Sinclair, 1994). By removing some of the mystery, community corrections can dispel some of the related fears.

Performance-Based Measures

Process and outcome measures are particularly important when initiating new programs and practices that are very different in nature from those typically performed. Following are examples of performance-based measures that can be used to determine if victim services are being implemented as designed, and how effectively these services are meeting informational and other needs and interests of crime victims.

Process Measures

Percent of Victim Impact Statements Completed. A victim impact statement provides the

Figure 54 - Percent of Victim Impact Statements Completed

Objective: A victim impact statement will be completed for 95% of all offenses that involved a victim.

Data Elements: Number of offenders convicted of a crime involving a victim, number of victim impact statements completed.

Formula: (Number of victim impact statements completed ÷ number of offenders convicted of a crime involving a victim) x 100.

Example: 1,019 offenders convicted of crimes that involved a victim were assigned to the department. In 988 cases, a victim impact statement was completed.

(988 ÷ 1019) x 100 = 97% **Objective was achieved!!!**

Figure 55 - Extent of Planning and Implementation to Address Victims' Needs

Objective: 80% of the case files reviewed for victim service planning and implementation during FY 1994 will be rated as "fully implemented."

Data elements: Number of cases reviewed, number of cases rated as fully implemented.

Formula: Number of cases rated as fully implemented ÷ number of cases reviewed x 100.

Example: 5%, or 49, of the cases in which a victim impact statement was completed (n = 988) were reviewed during FY 1994. 33 were rated as "fully implemented."

(33 ÷ 49) x 100 = 67%. **Objective was not achieved.**

opportunity for the victim to express how the criminal act affected their life. Information is requested regarding the financial, emotional, physical, and psychological impacts of the crime. Probation/parole officers often evaluate the victim's statements and provide the information to decisionmakers for consideration. Additionally, officers sometimes make recommendations for ways in which a victim's needs and interests can be met including the payment of restitution, the performance of community service, or the imposition of protection orders. By documenting the number of victim impact statements completed, agencies can demonstrate their commitment to addressing the needs and concerns of crime victims.

<u>Extent to which Plans and Services Are Implemented to Address Victims' Needs</u>. An agency may choose to take the above process

measure one step further and evaluate the extent to which plans and services are actually implemented to address victims' needs as identified through victim impact statements. Just as offender case plans should be individualized, so should services designed to meet victims' specific needs. Some victims want to be notified about offender movement through the system, while others do not want to be reminded. Some victims may desire information on available treatment and services to address issues related to their victimization. Some victims may qualify for state funded compensation and need information on application procedures. Some victims may have particular requests regarding arrangements for the payment of restitution. These diverse factors should lead to diverse strategies for meeting victim needs. To determine the extent to which plans and services are implemented to meet victims' needs, supervisors could use a case audit procedure similar to that used to determine the extent to which case plans and supervision addresses an offender's risks and needs. Such a process would reinforce the agency's goal of remaining sensitive to victims' concerns and informational needs.

Outcome Measures

Proportion of Restitution and/or Court Fees Collected. Agencies often report the dollar amount of restitution that is collected. To say that jurisdiction A collected $100,000 in restitution last year does not communicate the extent to which victims' losses were recovered or the extent to which offenders kept pace with payment schedules. A better outcome measure is the *proportion* of restitution collected. The total amount of restitution collected could be reported in conjunction with the proportion of restitution

collected. Reporting that Jurisdiction A collected $100,000 in restitution last year, representing 75 percent of the restitution ordered by judges in the jurisdiction, places the figure in perspective.

The amount of restitution ordered and/or collected is only part of the picture. The amount of restitution ordered is often based on the offender's ability to pay and not the amount of loss sustained by the victim. To compensate for this discrepancy between the amount of actual loss and the amount of restitution ordered, an agency may elect to establish a goal to increase the percent of victim losses recovered.

Extent of Victim Satisfaction with Services and Department. Victims are key stakeholders

Figure 56 - Proportion of Restitution Collected

Objective: 75% of all restitution scheduled to be paid according to offender payment plans during 1994 will be collected by year end 1994.

Data elements: Total amount of restitution payments scheduled to be paid by offenders during 1994, total amount of restitution collected during 1994.

Formula: (Total amount of restitution collected during 1994 ÷ total amount of restitution payments scheduled to be paid during 1994) x 100.

Example: During 1994, offenders were scheduled to make restitution payments totalling $148,200. $94,848 of this restitution was actually collected.

($94,848 ÷ $148,200) x 100 = 64% **Objective was not achieved.**

Figure 57 - Extent of Victim Satisfaction with Agency Victim Services

Objective: 80% of crime victims will rate agency victim services satisfactory at the time the offender completes supervision or has his/her community supervision revoked.

Data elements: Number of victim surveys rated satisfactory or higher, number of surveys administered.

Formula: Number of victim surveys rated satisfactory or higher ÷ number of surveys administered x 100

Example: 231 victims were asked to complete a "victim satisfaction" survey during the first quarter of 1994. 178 surveys were returned. 121 surveys rated the department's victim services programs as satisfactory.

(121 ÷ 178) x 100 = 68% of victims were satisfied with the departments victims services. **Objective was not achieved.**

in community corrections. As with all stake-holders in the system, the extent of satisfaction with services and the department should be assessed. The results of this effort will assist administrators in improving the services that are provided to crime victims.

The department could develop a survey to be completed by the victim at the time an offender completes supervision requirements. The responses from such an instrument will provide information on the degree of victim satisfaction and other information that can be used to improve victim services in the agency.

Conclusion

Victim services are likely to become an integral component of community corrections agencies. Providing victim services reflects a comprehensive approach to addressing the problems of crime within communities. It assists probation and parole officers in remaining sensitive to victims' needs *and* in making offenders understand the negative impacts of their behavior. The collection of restitution is just one example of how instrumental community corrections agencies can be in compensating victims for their losses. By acknowledging victims' needs and concerns, notifying them of important case activity, and educating them about community corrections' mission, agencies can alleviate some of the fear and confusion associated with their victimization.

Reaching out to victims represents a specific attempt to involve citizens in the mission of community corrections. The next chapter discusses another avenue for broadening the spectrum of individuals and agencies involved in community corrections -- the coordination and promotion of community services as a means of addressing offender needs.

CHAPTER EIGHT

COORDINATE AND PROMOTE USE OF COMMUNITY SERVICES

> **Goal:**   The Anytown, USA Community Corrections Department will coordinate and promote the use of community services to make full use of available services in the community to meet the needs of its offenders.

Introduction

Three-quarters of all convicted offenders will serve all or part of their sentence in the community under the supervision of probation and parole officers. On the average in 1992, a probation officer with a regular caseload supervised 124 probationers (Camp & Camp, 1993). Because of time and energy constraints, the extent to which probation and parole officers can supervise offenders is limited. Without a network of individuals and services within the community, offenders would not get the services required for risk control and reform. This chapter focuses on the importance of coordinating services within the community and the active role that probation and parole officers and agencies can take to encourage that coordination. Several process and outcome measures are discussed that reflect the extent to which they are successful.

Rationale for Goal

Offenders under the supervision of community corrections agencies require a variety of services throughout their rehabilitative process. While these services are increasingly being provided in-house, probation and parole agencies are still dependent on other community service providers to meet these needs. Cooperative planning between probation/parole and other community

services is essential. An important step in cooperative planning is the ability for both systems to share information and resources. Information can be integrated by sharing files and previous assessments, as well as professional opinions and perceptions.

As Faegre and Glenn (1978) point out, each of the systems has strengths and weaknesses. "The power and accountability of the criminal justice system can help push offenders into treatment and keep them there" whereas "the treatment system can balance control and support on the one hand with the potential for growth and development on the other, always gauging the ability and the readiness of the offender to assume greater control over his own life." Coordination offers the opportunity of combining the strengths of each system so they work together, compensating for the shortcomings inherent in the other system.

Coordinating services can be difficult and complex. While community corrections and treatment providers have common goals (e.g., rehabilitation, promote a drug free lifestyle), the differences in terminology and philosophical orientations can lead to goal confusion and misunderstandings. Cooperation begins with mutual understanding which requires learning about the operational issues, activities, and philosophies of each organization.

Coordinating services is rapidly complicated when rules and regulations provide what are perceived to be formidable barriers (e.g., confidentiality regulations) between probation/parole and community service providers. For example, probation and parole agencies often request drug test results as a part of the progress reports for offenders referred to drug treatment. Treatment providers often consider drug test results to be a part of the information included in patient/offender privileges. Disagreement also arises around the issue of who should be treated. Because criminal justice referrals are often without resources and motivation, they are not typically the favored offender. Often they are found "not amenable to treatment" and refused services. These issues and the resource constraints that all community agencies are experiencing should make it clear that mere co-existence is not sufficient. Cooperative, reciprocal relationships among community corrections and other service providers are a necessity. The next section discusses activities performed by probation/parole agencies to cultivate these relationships.

Probation and Parole Activities

Conducting a Resource/Needs Assessment

The first step in planning for offender services is to conduct a needs assessment. A needs assessment involves gathering information on:

- the criminogenic needs of offenders including the extent of the problem and possible causes;

- current solutions and resources for addressing the problems; and

- the extent of unmet needs.

In addition to the data on offender needs, data should be gathered on community programs and resources to determine both the availability and the quality of services. The following information should be collected on each service provider:

- the range and type of services offered;

- profile of staff;

- cost of services;

- type and level of agency funding;

- physical accessibility of services;

- profile of offenders served;

- profile of offenders refused for treatment;

- problems encountered by current program participants;

- time lags between referrals and treatment; and

- evaluation results of services rendered (Maddock, Daley & Moss, 1988).

This information can be obtained from public officials, employees of the community resources themselves, employees of other community service organizations (e.g., juvenile and domestic relations courts, welfare agencies), and from recipients of the services.

The needs assessment process should indicate which needs are not being met due to a lack of available services or due to poor quality services. The remaining activities provide mechanisms for cultivating needed services.

Keep Agencies and the Public Informed of Offender Needs

Probation/parole agencies routinely conduct assessments of offenders under their supervision to determine their needs. Periodically, the assessment information should be analyzed and summarized. Emerging trends and/or change(s) in areas of need should be documented and shared with other service providers in the community. The information could be used by community service providers to change existing programs or develop new programs to better meet the needs of their prospective program participants. These results should be shared with other key stakeholders as well. Documented needs among the offender population can be used to justify additional resources and programming.

Prepare Interagency Agreements

The provision of effective services to offenders is dependent on the support and cooperation from other community service providers. To ensure that agencies clearly understand their respective roles and responsibilities it is recommended that interagency agreements be prepared. Key elements of an interagency agreement include:

• a joint purpose statement;
• a description of treatment and services provided;
• the population to be served;
• methods of referral;
• criteria for accepting/rejecting referred offenders;
• methods for assessing offender needs;
• confidentiality issues;
• frequency and type of client contact;
• frequency and type of contact between agencies;
• success and failure criteria; and

• provisions for periodic review and modification (APPA and the National Association of State Alcohol and Drug Abuse Directors, 1992).

Interagency agreements facilitate cooperation between community corrections agencies and other service providers. Most importantly, however, interagency agreements ensure that services are available for properly identifying and addressing offender needs.

Maintain Contact with Agencies

Open lines of communication are necessary to insure that there is interagency cooperation. Regular meetings between probation/parole personnel and community service providers should be conducted to clarify roles and responsibilities. If possible, probation/parole representatives should participate on community service agencies' advisory boards as ex officio members. Representatives of community service providers could be asked to participate as members of probation/parole advisory boards. Regular communication regarding individual offenders is imperative for keeping abreast of progress and problems. Procedures for such communication should be established upfront.

Participate in Multi-Disciplinary Teams

Since many offenders' problems are multi-faceted, they require a multi-disciplinary response in order to provide comprehensive and coordinated prevention and intervention services. A multi-disciplinary team is a functioning unit composed of professional and/or representatives of service agencies who work together to communicate, collaborate, and consolidate knowledge from which plans are made, actions determined, and future decisions influenced (Brill, 1976). In some situations a multi-disciplinary team may be established to effectively diagnose offender problems. In addition to diagnosis, multi-disciplinary teams identify and coordinate appropriate community resources, discover gaps in the availability of needed resources, and participate in related educational and service projects.

Performance-Based Measures

In trying to keep up with the workload associated with the high caseloads typical of today's community corrections agencies, interagency coordination often becomes a low priority. Establishing measurable performance standards reminds agency personnel of the importance of these activities. Process and outcome measures such as those discussed below help agencies to assess the extent to which they are using the community resources available and the efforts they are making to coordinate and enhance these services.

Process Measures

Extent to Which Interagency Agreements are Implemented. An important component of interagency agreements is the evaluation of how well the agreement is working for the respective parties. Are referrals being made as outlined in the agreement? Are offenders being assessed according to the stated methods? Is communication between the two agencies occurring as agreed? These and other questions should be explored periodically to determine if the process outlined in the interagency agreement is being implemented as designed. Identifying strengths and weaknesses in the process will help agencies to understand why certain outcomes are produced and guide improvements.

Figure 58 - Degree of Interagency Agreement Implementation

Objective: 100% of interagency agreements between community corrections and community service agencies will result in ratings of "above average" or better.

Data Elements: Number of interagency agreements evaluated, number rated "above average" or better.

Example: During 1994, six interagency agreements were evaluated. Four of these agreements received ratings of "above average" or better.

Formula: (Number of agreements receiving ratings of "above average" or better ÷ number of agreements evaluated) x 100.

(4 ÷ 6) x 100 = 67%. **Objective was not achieved.**

Percent of Offenders Accepted/Rejected by Various Agencies. The percent of offenders accepted for services points to the degree of interagency cooperation and to the degree of available resources in the community. If the percent of rejections is high, three possible situations could exist: 1) the service provider may be inappropriately refusing service based on offender characteristics or lack of motivation; 2) adequate services may not exist to meet the needs of all offenders; and 3) referrals may not be appropriate. In all cases, agency personnel should work with community service providers to ensure that offenders are being appropriately referred and accepted for services. In the example provided, Anytown USA should work with key stakeholders in the community to develop additional service opportunities for the 17 percent of offenders rejected from services.

Figure 59 - Percent of Offenders Accepted by Various Agencies

Objective: 80% of offenders referred to the Mental Health Agency, will be accepted for services.

Data Elements: Number of offenders accepted for services, number of referrals made to the Mental Health Agency

Formula: (Number of offenders accepted for services ÷ number of referrals made to the Mental Health Agency) x 100

Example: During the first quarter of 1994, 280 referrals were made to the Mental Health Agency. 232 offender referrals were accepted for services.

(232 ÷ 280) x 100 = 83% of all referrals were accepted for services **Objective was achieved.**

Outcome Measures

Progress of Offenders in Community Service Agencies. After an offender has been admitted to a community service program, it is the role of the probation/parole agency to track their progress. Tracking an offender's progress will involve direct communication with the service provider. Attendance and the service provider's assessment of the offender's progress should be documented.

For example, an offender assigned to an Alcoholics Anonymous group may be tracked on the basis of the number of sessions attended per week. Another offender assigned to an in-patient drug treatment provider may be tracked on the basis of the counselor's assessment of progress. In some situations, the offender's progress could be tracked through the number

Figure 60 - Progress of Offenders in Community Service Agencies

Objective: 80% of all offenders participating in the Substance Abuse Outpatient Treatment Program during 1994 will make satisfactory progress in service programs as measured by monthly progress reports containing information on attendance, the counselor's assessment of progress and urinalyses results.

Data Elements: Number of offenders with satisfactory program progress, number of offenders participating in service agencies.

Formula: (Number of offenders with satisfactory program progress ÷ number of offenders participating in service agencies) x 100

Example: During 1994, 475 offenders participated in the Substance Abuse Outpatient Treatment Program. 365 offenders demonstrated satisfactory progress.

(335 ÷ 475) x 100 = 71% of the offenders demonstrated satisfactory progress in services provided by community service agencies. **Objective was not achieved.**

and frequency of positive urinalysis. The combination of all three of these indicators would provide a more complete and accurate assessment of the offender's progress and the community service agency's overall effectiveness.

Percent of Offenders Satisfactorily Completing Services. Another outcome measure that indicates the appropriate use and delivery of services, is the percent of offenders successfully completing the service(s). Too often, offenders lack the motivation to complete the service, or they continue their criminal activities and are incarcerated. Higher retention and completion

Figure 61 - Percent of Offenders Satisfactorily Completing Service

Objective: 60% of all offenders referred to domestic violence treatment will satisfactorily complete the program.

Data Elements: Number of offenders referred to services, number of offenders successfully completing services.

Formula: (Number of offenders who satisfactory completed services ÷ number of offenders referred x 100

Example: 167 offenders were referred to domestic violence treatment during 1994. 87 were successfully discharged.

(87 ÷ 167) x 100 = 52% of offenders satisfactorily completed domestic violence treatment programs during 1994. **Objective was not achieved.**

rates can signify effective agency practices. Perhaps stronger lines of communication between the probation/parole agency and the service provider contributes to higher success rates. Or perhaps success can be attributed to better offender/treatment matching within a specific agency. These and other factors should be explored as a means of determining which practices lead to higher rates of retention and completion.

Conclusion

Offenders, assigned to community supervision, have many needs that must be met if they are to return as productive members of society. Given limited resources, probation/parole agencies must work cooperatively with community service providers to secure needed services for their offenders. While community corrections and community service providers often have common goals, the coordination of services can be difficult and complex. Sharing of information and resources is the first step in developing a mutual relationship that results in the offenders receiving the best services available in the community.

This chapter concludes the working model of performance-based measurement. The sample process and outcome measures provided within each chapter support the mission, goals and priorities of Anytown USA's Community Corrections Department. While agencies may choose to use many of these same measures, they are encouraged to conduct a similar exercise to that conducted by Anytown including:

• exploring the agency's values, mission and goals;

• examining the philosophies upon which goals and activities are based; and

• identifying performance-based measures that assess and communicate what it is that the agency does and how well they do it.

The work does not stop here. Establishing a performance-based measurement strategy is certainly a good first step. The next step is to make the strategy work for the agency. The next module talks about how a performance-based measurement strategy can guide program operations and improvements. Only when agencies set performance standards, measure the degree of achievement, *and* respond to the results can they be considered a learning organization that is open to challenges and organizational growth.

MODULE III

COMMUNITY CORRECTIONS
AS A LEARNING ORGANIZATION

MODULE III

COMMUNITY CORRECTIONS AS A LEARNING ORGANIZATION

Module Overview

Change, in any form, produces anxiety and discomfort. Uncontrolled, irrational change can be utterly frightening. Controlled, rational and purposeful change can stimulate positive growth. This third and final module captures the primary values of a performance-based measurement strategy -- it describes how a performance-based measurement strategy:

- guides agencies and their personnel through the change process;
- provides agencies with a vision, a logical well-planned pathway;
- allows agencies and their personnel to learn and grow; and
- leads to a healthy, vital organization.

Module I described the importance of involving staff in the development of a performance-based measurement strategy. *Chapter Nine: Measuring Staff Performance* discusses the importance of holding staff accountable for these performance measures. It describes how management practices and performance-based measurements can assuage the threat of accountability by setting clear expectations and standards. This chapter reviews the challenges of evaluating staff performance and shows how performance-based measurements can assist managers in maximizing staff resources.

Chapter Ten: Analyzing, Reporting, and Applying Results explores the final phase in the cyclical process of performance-based measurement. This final phase is not to be confused with the end; the feedback from performance-based measurements opens the door to new challenges and continued organizational growth. Analyzing and reporting results highlights positive outcomes, uncovers ineffective practices, and guides agencies to explore alternative methods for achieving organizational goals. If properly implemented a system of performance-based measurement will keep agencies at the vanguard of community corrections practices.

CHAPTER NINE

MEASURING STAFF PERFORMANCE

Introduction

Focusing on processes and outcomes as indicators of effectiveness, such as those outlined in Module II, should change the nature of many operations within community corrections organizations. Employee performance evaluations will change dramatically in terms of performance criteria, employee/supervisor interaction, and corrective actions. Staff will now be held accountable for the quality of what they do and the results they achieve, rather than for the number of times they do something. Being held accountable for results can be a frightening prospect for employees at all levels of the organization. But if staff are not held accountable for results, performance-based measurements are of very little use. This chapter will discuss the complexities associated with staff evaluations within the context of performance-based measurements and the benefits that can be realized.

Linking Employee Evaluations
to Performance-Based Measurement

Petersilia (1993) has stated, "once the agency has identified its goals and the methods it uses to address each goal, it can specify objective (measurable) criteria that determine the extent to which the activities are being performed." She describes the completion of presentence investigations, hypothetically, as an activity identified to achieve a mission-driven goal of assessing the offender's suitability for placement. Performance measures may include process measures designed to determine if services are being delivered as planned (e.g., the accuracy and completeness of the investigation), or outcome measures designed to determine if the output had

an impact on results (e.g., appropriate placement in community supervision as measured by offender success). As discussed in Chapter Two, both measures are necessary -- outcomes are only meaningful if the processes occurred as planned.

The employees of an organization are responsible for planning and delivering services or products. As stated earlier in this monograph "what gets measured gets done" (Osborne & Gaebler, 1993, p. 146). Programs that do not pay careful attention to closely aligning employee evaluations with process and outcome requirements should not expect to see the program implemented as designed or the desired goals achieved.

Linking measures of employee performance to process and outcome measures is not a simple matter. Challenges in evaluating staff performance include:

Criteria selection: Returning to the PSI example, what indicator of staff performance best supports the selected methods intended to achieve the desired outcome? Quantitative measures (e.g., number completed on time) are much simpler, but less helpful than qualitative measures which evaluate how the PSI meets the expectations of the court. An organization may realistically require multiple employee performance evaluations using distinctly different criteria instead of the "one size fits all" as common in most organizations.

Validity: Construct validity (i.e., does the criterion actually measure what it purports to measure?) is critical. Is it the number of referrals to treatment or the appropriateness of referrals to treatment that differentiates levels of staff performance (Hatry, 1981)? Face validity is also important. Agency administrators should try to identify performance indicators that staff believe are important. Selecting referrals to treatment as a measure of staff performance in an agency whose mission and values only deal with surveillance will lack credibility.

Inter-rater reliability: Inter-rater reliability refers to the consistency of an instrument's use from one individual to another. One problem with most employee performance systems is that they are subjective. For any given employee, a criterion may be viewed as positive or not, depending upon the evaluator. Instead of supporting organizational goals, this type of evaluation reflects who is doing the evaluation, not the performance that is being discussed. Oversight reviews, in which a sample of completed performance evaluations are reviewed, may help ensure consistency where the evaluation process is sufficiently objective and well designed. Otherwise another layer of subjectivity is added.

Increasing objectivity is not without problems, however. One ineffective approach is to reduce performance to only those things that can be quantified (e.g., numbers of contacts, number of drug tests conducted). In one example, an agency separated an offender interview and case planning process into activities supervisors could count and read. The result was that officers focused on activities rather than on the process and desired outcomes. Performance as measured appeared to increase, but overall quality actually declined. Reducing complex processes to discrete, quantifiable activities may result in absurd measures which provide no meaningful performance information and prevent staff from "seeing the forest for the trees."

Time frame: The primary purpose of evaluations is to provide staff with feedback which will

encourage a level of proficiency in implementing outcome oriented methods and activities. Trying to obtain real time performance data is a problem which most evaluation methods share. The late W. Edwards Demming (1986), quality guru, likened staff evaluations based on management by objectives (MBO) to trying to figure out where you are going by riding backwards on a horse. Feedback from performance evaluations, which are typically done annually, focuses on performance in the past.

Frequency of evaluation: Feedback from performance evaluations is more likely to be relevant the more frequently the process occurs. The trade off is that the administrative costs -- staff time -- increase with frequency.

Ease of administration: As attempts are made to deal with issues such as subjectivity, the evaluation may become increasingly complex. This may increase the duration and frequency of performance evaluations. A simple example would be measuring compliance with program contact standards. If maximum cases require three face-to-face contacts per month, measuring performance for this indicator every six months is not difficult. If, on the other hand, reduction in drug/alcohol use among officers' caseloads is the measurement used, performance measures are challenging. Another downside to increased complexity are errors by the evaluator due either to honest mistakes or sabotage of what is seen as a flawed process. If it is too difficult supervisors will not do it, and if it is too simple no one should do it.

The Threat of Accountability

Effective case planning with offenders focuses on the desired behavior or the desired outcome, and outlines specific action steps toward achieving that outcome (Clear & O'Leary, 1983). Attending treatment, while to be encouraged, does not excuse an offender's continued drug and alcohol abuse. The same principle applies to employee and organizational performance. Conducting fifty face-to-face contacts per week should not excuse an extremely low rate of restitution collection, a high rate of drug and alcohol abuse, or a high absconding rate within an officer's caseload.

Officers become concerned when they are being held accountable for offender change, stating that they can "provide opportunity for offender change" but that they have no control over whether the change actually occurs. While this may be a valid concern, what must be remembered, is that officers and organizations are already being held responsible for offender change, or lack thereof, with the current focus on recidivism as the sole criteria of program success. The scheme proposed here merely gives officers more realistic targets to strive for and a chance to highlight the positive outcomes achieved with offenders every day. It also provides them with an opportunity to learn which practices are linked to success.

Growing pains are inevitable throughout this process. There are, however, ways to ease the discomfort. Managers can promote buy-in and minimize skepticism by involving officers in developing the performance-based measurements and listening to their concerns. Management must also commit the necessary training and resources required for achieving the results for which staff will be held accountable. Most importantly, it should be made clear that accountability will be required at all organizational levels including line, managerial, and administrative levels. Being held accountable for results should be presented and perceived as an opportunity for professional growth rather than as a threat to the status quo. Managers must lead the organization through the rough spots.

Promoting Accountability through a System of Rewards

Incentive systems provide a potent method for promoting accountability and positive performance. Government agencies have been fairly negligent in rewarding staff for their performance, partially because of the subjective nature of performance evaluations, and partially because of fiscal constraints. Performance-based measurement resolves this first issue by lending itself to specific performance standards which can be used as a gauge for identifying outstanding performance. For example, in a hypothetical jurisdiction, increasing the educational level of offenders has been established as an organizational priority through clearly defined mission, goals and objectives. When comparing officer performance by examining such indicators as rate of school attendance, class hours completed, improved grades, and number obtaining their GED or other certification of completion, it is revealed that an officer has successfully facilitated educational improvements among eighty percent of her caseload as compared to 30-50 percent improvements among other similar caseloads. By rewarding her for this outstanding performance, a manager demonstrates commitment to this organizational priority and promotes continued accountability for the educational improvements of offenders.

The second issue is not as easily resolved; there are, however, many ways to reward staff for positive performance with little budgetary impact. Such incentives could include:
- recognition through certificates, plaques, newsletters or ceremonies;
- special parking privileges;
- increased autonomy;
- prioritization for training resources;
- additional skill building opportunities;
- nominations for regional or national awards and special recognition by professional associations; and

- opportunity for lateral career movement.

Agency personnel should be involved in the development of an incentives program. After all, they know best what would motivate them to achieve. Furthermore, by participating in the development of such a program, staff would become aware of the difficulties associated with providing incentives within extreme fiscal constraints and be more appreciative of, and motivated by, non-monetary rewards.

Impact of Management Practices

The vast majority of staff will perform adequately given proper direction and resources. Most examples of unsatisfactory performance within any given process are attributable to poor planning, training, or management. For example, management audits of a large urban community corrections office revealed a disparity in how risk/need classifications were completed. Reviews of case files in all offices revealed a pattern; something was systematically causing officers to misclassify cases. Further examination determined that the regional supervisor was very controlling and afraid of new information. If he did not understand policies issued by the main office he would not give the information to his staff -- so they continued to complete the classification process incorrectly. The lesson is, that while staff performance must be linked to other types of process evaluations, process failure is usually linked to management failure, not to the failure of individual staff.

Quality Control[1]

Supervisors can engage in quality control by establishing specific performance standards for officers to meet. This is a difficult concept for public organizations, specifically for those that deal with human behavior. However, quality control is essential because offender populations pose a risk to the public, and mistakes made in

the supervision of these populations can have serious repercussions for the offender, the agency and the community. Therefore, it is very important that officers stay focused on goals and results. Establishing specific performance standards for officers is one means to achieve this end.

Realistic performance standards can be developed by aggregating offender objectives within a caseload or a supervision unit and assessing their achievement. In establishing performance standards for each officer the supervisor will need to take into account the officer's strengths and weaknesses, the difficulty of the caseload, and the environment within which the officer has to work. For instance, in an area with a high unemployment rate it would be unrealistic to establish a performance standard of increasing caseload employment by 20 percent. Likewise, if an officer's caseload consists of predominantly chronically drug-involved offenders, a realistic goal for the caseload may be to increase the percentage of offenders drug free for 30 days by five percent. The point of establishing performance standards for each officer is to help the officers remain focused on the desired results and to facilitate learning with respect to discovering innovative or better methods for achieving results.

Establishing specific performance standards is also helpful in that it provides information on which officers appear to work best with specific kinds of cases. The data in Table 6 reveals that Officers Smith and Wilson appear to be working well with cases having employment objectives. There may be other officers who work well with substance abuse cases, sex offender cases, or assaultive offenders. With this information, the supervisor can assign cases to officers based upon their objectives-based performance and expertise. This can lead to enhanced organizational performance and the effective allocation of staff resources. By engaging in these activities,

Table 6 - Percent of Objectives Achieved

Officer	No. of Cases with Employment Objectives	Percent of Objectives Achieved
Smith	55	85
Jones	42	53
Baker	36	41
Wilson	48	63
Thomas	51	51
Watson	40	47

Source: Clear, T. R., & O'Leary, V. (1983). *Controlling the offender in the community.* Lexington, MA: Lexington Books.

the supervisor continually reinforces and aligns the decisions made by line officers toward achievement of results.

Conclusion

People are an organization's greatest resource. Given the proper learning environment and structured feedback on meaningful performance criteria, staff will work to improve outcomes and achieve desired goals. The more control people are given over their work, the more motivated, productive and effective they are. Using performance-based measurement in staff evaluations gives them that control. It allows for creative approaches to goal achievement rather than prescribed approaches and quantitative standards. It provides meaningful feedback on their work -- evidence of their worth to the offender, the organization and the community.

[1.] The information presented here was adapted from:

Clear, T. & O'Leary, V. (1983). *Controlling the offender in the community.* Lexington, MA: Lexington Books.

CHAPTER TEN

ANALYZING, REPORTING, AND APPLYING RESULTS

Introduction

Successful organizations are constantly learning, improving, and changing to meet the needs of their consumers. IBM would not exist today if they had ignored the personal computer market in favor of the status quo mainframe computers. Government agencies must borrow this page from the private sector's book. Performance-based measures help to meet this need by providing a credible source of information and knowledge about the effectiveness of programs and practices.

While measuring results is a good first step, just knowing that a problem exists is not enough. Until results are acted upon, community corrections organizations will remain stagnant. Results must be analyzed and communicated to interested stakeholders. Learning "what works" is a continuous, long-term process of testing, modifying, and retesting. Chapter Nine demonstrated how performance-based measures provide a direct link between officer performance and an agency's mission and goals. This chapter takes this one step further, and discusses the importance of translating performance-based measures into positive organizational growth.

Taking the Bad with the Good

What if performance-based measures contain bad news? One way to prepare is to anticipate results that are unfavorable (Blalock, 1990). Agencies that pursue performance measures as "proof" that their methods "work" set the stage for certain disappointment. If, however, an organization adopts the view that "feedback," rather than "proof" is the objective, disappoint-

ing results become an opportunity to examine alternatives. These may range from minor program changes to the elimination of the program. The very essence of performance-based measurement is that it provides a method for uncovering ineffective practices or programs.

For example, in the case of Anytown, USA the following two results should cause agencies to explore practices and programs to identify contributing factors:

1) **64 percent of all restitution scheduled to be paid according to offender payment plans during 1994 was actually collected (eleven percent lower than the stated objective).** This result should be of major concern to community corrections administrators. The collection of restitution serves many important purposes; it holds offenders accountable for their criminal behavior and reimburses victims for their monetary losses. Low rates of restitution collection undermine these two critical objectives of community supervision. Practices should be examined to determine where the problem lies. Are payment schedules set too low? Is noncompliance with restitution orders being addressed? Are offenders being released from supervision prematurely? Once discovered, program modifications should be made and the appropriate staff training should occur. Results should again be documented to determine if the modifications corrected the problem.

2) **The overall attendance rate for offenders participating in the community outpatient treatment program was 59 percent (16 percent lower than the stated objective).**

Low attendance rates are cause for concern for several reasons. First, they indicate noncompliance with court orders. Second, they lead one to question the offenders' whereabouts. Third, and most importantly, low attendance rates may lead to low rates of success in treatment; participation in treatment has been found to be positively correlated to program success (Anglin & Hser, 1990; Jolin & Stipak, 1992). Low attendance rates could be due to individual problems with offenders. Transportation and child care are often cited problems for treatment absences. In rural areas especially, transportation is a legitimate problem and one that may be resolved with assistance from community corrections personnel or volunteers. Another potential contributor to low attendance rates may be the failure of probation and parole or treatment personnel to respond to noncompliance. Sanctioning from either organization may "encourage" attendance. A third possibility may be a lack of communication between agencies so that no one is aware of the offender's status and absences are not addressed.

Reasons for poor outcomes must be explored. Community corrections agencies and personnel cannot continue to avoid responsibility for poor outcomes. Probation and parole originated with the idea that people can change. Tax dollars are provided to probation and parole agencies to serve as a conduit to that change. When dealing with human behavior, 100 percent certainty or 100 percent success is unrealistic. But by testing, modifying, and retesting programs and practices, community corrections agencies and professionals can begin to develop a sound knowledge base about "what works."

Searching for Answers

People frequently complain about "bad data." What they often mean is that the data is not useful, does not support their methods, or is inconclusive. But a story generally lies behind the numbers. This is particularly true when measuring processes. For example, it is not uncommon to find wide variation in the implementation of processes and programs between two offices in one district. Plausible explanations for the variation need to be confirmed or disputed based on process evaluation data.

When the performance data does not provide clear direction, agencies and personnel must rely on several sources of knowledge to guide further exploration and decisions: common knowledge, theoretical support, and empirical evidence. Common knowledge is practical information that is gained from experience. Many practices are widely accepted by the profession as "the way things are done." Common knowledge should be used as a basis for further exploration, rather than as an excuse to accept the status quo. Theoretical support comes in the form of assumptions or speculation about a particular phenomena and provides a framework for analyzing, predicting, or explaining an occurrence. Empirical evidence is proof or verification of something through observation or experiment. Empirical evidence from related areas may be drawn upon to support a particular decision or direction. These sources of knowledge, and the knowledge created by performance-based measurement, can assist agencies in unraveling the mysteries to success in community corrections.

Who to Tell and How

It is one thing to obtain data; it is quite another to explain it in a way that is both technically correct and useful. Most organizations will rely on internal or external experts at some point when conducting evaluations (please see Appendix A for information on evaluation protocol). Researchers, consultants, and staff who care about their customers will take care to make the information credible and understandable. Staff should be educated to be conversant regarding the relationship between measurement, process, and outcomes.

Key stakeholders within the criminal justice system and the community at large should be informed of agency and program outcomes on a regular basis. Periodic reports and statistics on probation and parole operations, will give decision makers a clearer picture of what resources are available and how they are distributed. An understanding of departmental constraints may lead to increased stakeholder support for both daily operations, such as sentencing recommendations within a PSI, and big picture considerations such as the need for additional financial and human resources.

As discussed in Chapter One, measuring outcomes reflects what an agency values and communicates clearly what the agency does. An honest, straightforward approach to reporting outcomes is essential. Poor results should not be hidden behind technical and statistical jargon. It is always best to control information from the inside, rather than leaving its interpretation to someone who knows little about the system.

How data is reported should be determined by the audience for whom it is intended. Sharing both positive and negative outcomes will earn greater respect and credibility with all audiences. Measuring performance demonstrates a commitment to improved practices; and key information about agency struggles may elicit support and assistance for those improvements. The amount and format of information should be carefully considered. The usefulness of long, comprehensive reports is most likely limited to agency personnel who are directly impacted by their contents. Legislators and judges may prefer only receiving information that impacts their decision making process. The information should be concise and, wherever possible, in graphic form. An example of such a report

appears in Appendix C. Excerpts from the Annual Report of Anytown, USA highlight the key results in a crisp, clear format. Important information about the agency's accomplishments can be quickly gleaned from the report. Information presented in a useable, reader-friendly format is more likely to gain the desired attention and support.

Conclusion

Through the appropriate analysis, reporting, and application of results community corrections can demonstrate their commitment to achieving their stated goals. Successful agencies are those that are actively involved in learning. They pursue information and work to enhance their knowledge base. They modify, adapt, and accept the challenges that come with change and growth. Community corrections agencies who fully participate in performance-based measurement have much to gain and even more to contribute.

The past decade has brought incredible challenges to community corrections. Agencies and practitioners have demonstrated a commitment to enhancing their programs and services and searching for better ways to do things. As a profession, community corrections must continue to elevate their knowledge and skills. A system of performance-based measurements will facilitate this professional and organizational growth. By demonstrating results community corrections agencies can position themselves as agencies that make a difference in the safety of American communities.

REFERENCES

REFERENCES

Abadinsky, H. (1991). *Probation and parole: Theory and practice.* Englewood Cliffs, New Jersey: Prentice Hall.

American Bar Association. (1970). *Standards relating to probation.* Chicago: Author.

American Correctional Association. (1966). *Manual of Correctional Standards.* College Park, Maryland: Author.

American Probation and Parole Association. (1994a). *Restructuring intensive supervision programs: Applying what works.* Lexington, KY: Author.

American Probation and Parole Association. (1994b). *A guide to enhancing victim services within probation and parole.* Lexington, KY: Author.

American Probation and Parole Association. (1993a). *American Probation and Parole Association membership update survey.* (Report prepared for APPA Board of Directors Meeting, January 31 - February 3, 1993, Austin, Texas). Lexington, KY: Author.

American Probation and Parole Association. (1993b). Probation and parole speaks out: A report on APPA's membership survey. *Perspectives, 17*(4), 44-45.

American Probation and Parole Association. (1991). *American Probation and Parole Association Board of Directors Manual.* Lexington, KY: Author.

American Probation and Parole Association and National Association of State Alcohol and Drug Abuse Directors. (1992). *Coordinated interagency drug training project: Participant manual.* Lexington, KY: Author.

American Probation and Parole Association and National Association of Probation Executives. (1988). *National narcotics intervention training program.* Lexington, KY.

Andrews, D. A. (1989). Recidivism is predictable and can be influenced: Using risk assessments to reduce recidivism. *Forum on Corrections Research, 1*(2), 11-17.

Andrews, D. A., Bonta, J., & Hoge, R. D. (1990). Classification for effective rehabilitation: Rediscovering psychology. *Criminal Justice and Behavior, 17*(10): 19-52.

Anglin, M. D., & Hser, Y. (1990). Treatment of drug abuse. In M. Tonry & J. Q. Wilson (Eds.), *Crime and Justice: Drugs and Crime* (pp. 355-375). Chicago, IL: University of Chicago.

Anonymous. (1982). *President's task force on victims of crime final report.*

Benekos, P. J. (1990, March). Beyond reintegration: Community corrections in a retributive era. *Federal Probation,* 52-56.

Blalock, A. B. (Ed.). (1990). *Evaluating social programs at the state and local level.* Kalamazoo, Michigan: W. E. Upjohn Institute for Employment Research.

Boone, H. N. (1994, Winter). An examination of recidivism and other outcome measures: A review of the literature. *Perspectives, 18*(1), 12-18.

Brill, N. I. (1976). *Teamwork: Working together in the human services.* Philadelphia, PA: J. B. Lippincott Company.

Byrne, J. M. (1989, July). Reintegrating the concept of community into community-based corrections. *Crime and Delinquency, 35*(3), 471-497.

Byrne, J. M., & Kelly, L. (1989). *Restructuring probation as an intermediate sanction: An evaluation of the Massachusetts Intensive Probation Supervision Program.* Final Report to the National Institute of Justice, Research Program on the Punishment and Control of Offenders. Washington, DC: U.S. Department of Justice.

Camp, G. M., & Camp, C. G. (1993). *The corrections yearbook: Probation and parole.* South Salem, New York: Criminal Justice Institute.

Castle, M. (1991). Alternative sentencing: Selling it to the public. *Research in Action.* Washington, DC: National Institute of Justice.

Clear, T. R., Clear, V. B., & Burrell, W. D. (1989). *Offender assessment and evaluation The presentence investigation report.* Cincinnati, Ohio: Anderson Publishing Co.

Clear, T. R., & Hardyman, P.L. (1990). The new intensive supervision movement. *Crime and Delinquency, 36,* 42-60.

Clear, T. R. & Latessa, E. (1993). Probation officer roles in intensive supervision: Surveillance versus treatment. *Justice Quarterly, 10,* 441.

Clear, T. R., & O'Leary, V. (1983). *Controlling the offender in the community.* Lexington, MA: Lexington Books.

Cochran, D. (1989, September). A practitioner's perspective. *Research in Corrections, 2,* 57-63.

Cochran, D., Corbett, Jr., R. P., Nidorf, B., Buck, G., & Stiles, D. (1991). *Managing probation with scarce resources: Obstacles and opportunities.* Washington, DC: National Institute of Corrections.

Cochran, D., Corbett, Jr., R. P., & Byrne, J. M. (1986, June). Intensive probation supervision in Massachusetts: A case study in change. *Federal Probation,* 32-41.

Corbett, R., Jr. (1989). Electronic monitoring. *Corrections Today, 6,* 74.

Covey, S. R. (1991). *Principle-centered leadership.* New York: Summit Books.

Crowe, A. H., & Schaefer, P. J. (1992). *Identifying and intervening with drug-involved youth.* Lexington, KY: American Probation and Parole Association.

Cullen, F. T., Cullen, J. B., & Wozniak, J. F. (1988). Is rehabilitation dead? The myth of the punitive public. *Journal of Criminal Justice, 16,* 303-317.

Cullen, F. T., & Gendreau, P. (1988). The effectiveness of correctional rehabilitation. In L. Goodstein and D.L. MacKenzie (Eds.), *The American Prison: Issues in Research Policy.* New York: Plenum.

Deming, W. E. (1986). *Out of the crisis.* Cambridge, MA: MIT.

DiIulio, Jr., J. J. (1992). *Rethinking the criminal justice system: Toward a new paradigm.* Washington, DC: U.S. Department of Justice.

Doble, J. (1987). *Crime and punishment: The public's view.* New York: Public Agenda Foundation.

Edna McConnel-Clark Foundation. (1993). *Americans behind bars.*

Erwin, B. S. (1990). Turning up the heat in Georgia. *Federal Probation, 2,* 17-24.

Erwin, B. S., & Bennett, L. A. (1987). *New dimensions in probation: Georgia's experience with intensive probation supervision (IPS).* Washington, DC: U.S. Department of Justice, National Institute of Justice.

Faegre, C. L., & Glen, H. S. (1978). *Justice treatment interface: A cross-discipline training course.* Rockville, MD: Department of Health, Education, and Welfare.

Fox, J. W. (1980). *Development of predictive factors for recidivism risk levels (Kentucky, 1979).* Richmond, KY: Eastern Kentucky University Department of Corrections. (NCJRS Document No. 076179).

Gendreau, P. (1994). Principles of effective intervention. In *Restructuring Intensive Supervision Programs: Applying What Works.* Lexington, KY: American Probation and Parole Association.

Gendreau, P., & Andrews, D.A. (1990). Tertiary prevention: What the meta-analyses of the offender treatment literature tell us about 'what works'. *Canadian Journal of Criminology, 32*, 173-184.

Gendreau, P., Cullen, F. T., & Bonta, J. (1994, Spring). Intensive rehabilitation supervision: The next generation in community corrections. *Federal Probation.*

Gendreau, P., & Ross, R.R. (1987). Revivification of rehabilitation: Evidence from the 1980s. *Justice Quarterly, 4*, 349-407.

Georgia Department of Corrections. (1993). *Catch the vision "Statement of values."* Atlanta, Georgia: Author.

Glaser, D. (1987). Classification for risk. In Gottfredson and Tonry (Eds.), *Prediction and Classification: Criminal Justice Decision Making.* Chicago: University of Chicago Press.

Good. (1993, December 27). Deeds in detention. *Dallas Morning News.*

Greene, R. (1988). Who's punishing whom? *Forbes, 121*(6), 132-133.

Harland, A. T. (1993). Defining a continuum of sanctions: Some research and policy development implications. In McGarry, P., & Carter, M. M. (Eds.), *The intermediate sanctions handbook: Experience and tools for policymakers* (pp. 35-40). Washington, D.C.: U.S. Department of Justice.

Harland, A.T., & Rosen, C.J. (1987). Sentencing theory and intensive supervision probation. *Federal Probation, LI*(4), 33-42.

Harris, K. M. (1984). Rethinking probation in the context of the justice model. In McAnany, Thomson and Fogel (Eds.) *Probation and Justice: Reconsideration of Mission.* Cambridge, Massachusetts: Oelgeschlager, Gunn and Hain, Publishers, Inc.

Harris, P. (1991). *Evaluation of criminal justice programs: Final report of technical assistance no. 92C1010 for the Community Justice Assistance Division of the Texas Department of Criminal Justice.* National Institute of Corrections.

Hatry, H. P., Winnie, R. E., & Fisk, D. M. (1981). *Practical program evaluation for state and local governments.* Washington, D.C.: Urban Institute Press.

Johnson, G., & Hunter, R. M. (1992). *Evaluation of the specialized drug offender program for the Colorado Judicial Department.* Boulder, Colorado: University of Colorado, Center for Action Research.

Jolin, A., & Stipak, B. (1992, April). Drug treatment and electronically monitored home confinement: An evaluation of a community-based sentencing option. *Crime and Delinquency, 38*(2), 158-170.

Kulis, C. J. (1983). Profit in the private presentence report. *Federal Probation, XVLII*(4), 11-15.

Langan, P. A., & Cunniff, M. A. (1992, February). *Recidivism of felons on probation, 1986-89.* Washington, D.C.: U.S. Department of Justice, Bureau of Justice Statistics. NCJ-134177.

Lawrence, R. (1991, October). Reexamining community corrections models. *Crime & Delinquency, 37*(4), 449-464.

Leukefeld, C., & Tims, F. (1988). Compulsory treatment: A review of findings. In Leukefeld and Tims (Eds.) *Compulsory Treatment of Drug Abuse: Research and Clinical Practice.* Rockville, MD: U.S. Department of Health and Human Services.

Lewis, R. G., and Greene, J. R. (1978). Implementation evaluation: A future direction in project evaluation. *Journal of Criminal Justice, 6*, 167-176.

Lindgren, S. A. (1992). Justice expenditure and employment, 1990. *Bureau of Justice Statistics Bulletin*. Washington, DC: U.S. Department of Justice.

Lipchitz, J. W. (1986, June). Back to the future: An historical view of intensive probation supervision. *Federal Probation,* 78-81.

Maddock, J. M., Daley, D., & Moss, H. B. (1988). A practical approach to needs assessment for chemical dependency programs. *Journal of Substance Abuse Treatment 5*.

Maloney, D., Romig, D., & Armstrong, T. (1988). Juvenile probation: The balanced approach. *Juvenile and Family Court Journal, 39*(3).

Maltz, M. D., & McCleary, R. (1977). The mathematics of behavioral change - Recidivism and construct validity. *Evaluation Quarterly, 1*(3), 421-438.

Markley, G. (1989, September). The marriage of mission, management, marketing, and measurement. *Research in Corrections, 2*, 49-56.

Maricopa County Adult Probation Department. (1993). *Celebrating today's successes and tomorrow's challenges: Annual report 1993*. Phoenix, Arizona: Author.

McClendon, B. W. (1992). *Customer service in local government*. Chicago: Planners Press, American Planning Association.

McDonald, D. C. (1995). *Managing Prison Health Care and Costs*. Washington, DC: National Institute of Justice.

McDonald, D. C. (1989). The cost of corrections: In search of the bottom line. *Research in Corrections, 2*(1), 1-25.

McGarry, P. (1993). The intermediate sanctions process: Rethinking your criminal justice system. In McGarry, P., & Carter, M. M. (Eds.), *The intermediate sanctions handbook: Experience and tools for policymakers* (pp. 11-14). Washington, D.C.: U.S. Department of Justice.

National Center for Juvenile Justice. (1991). *Desktop guide to good juvenile probation practice*. Washington, DC: Office of Juvenile Justice and Delinquency Prevention.

Nidorf, B. J. (1991, Summer). "Nothing works" revisited. *Perspectives, 15*(3), 12-13.

Office of National Drug Control Policy (1991). Cost of drug testing. *ONDCP Bulletin, 3*.

O'Leary, V. (1987, December). Probation: A system in change. *Federal Probation,* 8-11.

O'Leary, V., & Clear, T. (1984). *Directions for community corrections in the 1990s*. Washington, DC: National Institute of Corrections.

Osborne, D., & Gaebler, T. (1993). *Reinventing government*. New York: Plume.

Palmer, T. (1992). *The re-emergence of correctional intervention*. Newbury Park, California: Sage Publications, Inc.

Palmer, T. (1984, April). Treatment and role of classification: A review of basics. *Crime & Delinquency, 30*(2), 245-267.

Petersilia, J. (1993). *Measuring the performance of community corrections*. A paper prepared for the BJS-Princeton Outcomes Study Group.

Petersilia, J. (1990). Conditions that permit intensive supervision programs to survive. *Crime and Delinquency, 36*(1), 126-145.

Petersilia, J., Peterson, J., & Turner, S. (1992). *Evaluating intensive probation and parole supervision programs: Results of a nationwide experiment*. Unpublished Manuscript.

Petersilia, J., & Turner, S. (1993, May). *Evaluating intensive supervision probation/parole: Results of a nationwide experiment*. Washington, D.C.: U.S. Department of Justice, National Institute of Justice Research in Brief.

Petersilia, J., & Turner, S. (1990). *Intensive supervision for high-risk probationers: Findings from three California experiments*. California: RAND Corporation.

Ross, R., Fabiano, E., & Diemer-Ewles, C. (1988). Reasoning and rehabilitation. *International Journal of Offender Therapy and Comparative Criminology, 32,* 29-35.

Schuman, A. M. (1989). The cost of correctional services: Exploring a poorly charted terrain. *Research in Corrections, 2*(1), 27-33.

Sechrest, L., White, S. O., & Brown, E. D. (Eds.) (1979). *The rehabilitation of criminal offenders: Problems and prospects*. Washington, D.C.: National Academy of Sciences.

Shichor, D. (1992). Following the penological pendulum: The survival of rehabilitation. *Federal Probation, 2,* 19-25.

Sinclair, J. (1994). APPA's public hearings explore probation and parole's response to victims of crime: Speakers call for a new approach to victim issues. *Perspectives, 18*(3), 15-17.

Sutherland, E., & Cressey, D. (1966). *Principles of criminology*. New York: Lippincott.

Tilow, N. (1992, Winter). New public opinion poll cites support for intermediate punishment programs. *Perspectives,* 44-46.

Tonry, M. (1990, January). States and latent functions of ISP. *Crime and Delinquency, 36*(1), 174-191.

Turner, S., & Petersilia, J. (1992, February). Focusing on high-risk parolees: An experiment to reduce commitments to the Texas Department of Corrections. *Journal of Research in Crime and Delinquency, 29*(1), 34-61.

United States General Accounting Office. (1993). *Prison boot camps: Short-term prison costs reduced, but long-term impact uncertain*. Washington, DC: Author.

von Hirsch, A. (1976). *Doing justice: The report of the committee for the study of incarceration*. New York: Hill and Wang.

Wagner, D., & Baird, C. (1993). *Evaluation of the Florida Community Control Program*. (Report No. NCJ 137773). Washington, DC: National Institute of Justice.

Wagner, D. (1989, Summer). An evaluation of the high risk offender intensive supervision project. *Perspectives,* 22-27.

Waldo, G., & Griswold, D. (1979). Issues in the measurement of recidivism. In Sechrest, L., White, S. O., & Brown, E. D. (Eds.), *The rehabilitation of criminal offenders: Problems and Prospects* (pp. 225-250). Washington, D.C.: National Academy of Sciences.

APPENDIX A

AN ADMINISTRATOR'S GUIDE TO EVALUATION

AN ADMINISTRATOR'S GUIDE TO EVALUATION

"Researchers live in an ivory tower. Their only concern is publishing study results in obscure journals for other researchers to read. Their research has no practical implications for the average probation/parole professional."

"Practitioners aren't interested in research. They are only interested in doing things the same way they have always done them. If the 'sacred cow' programs are evaluated properly, they may be proven unsuccessful. They don't understand research methods and fail to cooperate fully with research efforts."

The preceding statements represent two opinions of research in community corrections. This adversarial relationship often exists because each of the parties fails to understand the role and responsibilities of the other party. If this type of adversarial relationship is allowed to exist between practitioners and evaluators, the advancement of the profession is sacrificed. Practitioners and evaluators are working for the same goal(s) and, with a little cooperation, they can assist each other in their efforts and advance the profession at the same time. Community corrections is not unique in the adversarial relationship between evaluators and practitioners. Other professions experience the same adversarial relationship between the practitioner and the academic researcher.

The purpose of this segment is to establish a protocol that can be used by evaluators and practitioners to ensure the full cooperation of all interested parties in achieving a common goal. The objective of the protocol will be to secure active participation of all interested stakeholders in the research process, especially at the development stages.

The protocol is built around a series of questions suggested by Brinkerhoff et al. (1983) in their book, *Program Evaluation*. The questions are designed direct a discussion which will insure that evaluators and stakeholders have a complete understanding of the evaluation process, and that

they have explored potential problems with the evaluation.

What is evaluation?

Many definitions of evaluation can be found in the literature. One well-know definition perceives evaluation as *the process of determining to what extent objectives are actually being realized* (Tyler, 1950, p. 69). Another widely accepted definition of evaluation is *providing information for decision makers* (Cronbach, 1963; Stufflebeam et al., 1971; and Alkin, 1969). A third definition of evaluation is *the systematic investigation of the worth or merit of some object* (Joint Committee, 1981, p. 12).

Types of evaluation

At this point a distinction needs to be made between the major types of evaluation. *Process evaluation* examines the individual components of the program to determine if they were implemented properly. Process evaluation can be proactive or retroactive. Proactive evaluation serves the decisionmaking process and is usually conducted while the program is being operated. Based upon the evaluation findings, changes can be made in the program to meet desired standards. Retroactive process evaluation also examines the individual components of a program, however, the examination occurs after the program has been completed. The purpose of retroactive evaluation is to provide program accountability.

Outcome evaluation examines indicators to determine the success or failure of a program. Outcome evaluation efforts usually start with a retroactive process evaluation to establish the creditability of the program. Only after the program's credibility has been established should attention be turned to the outcome evaluation.

The following example will be used to demonstrate process and outcome evaluation efforts. A urinalysis program was established to determine the extent of drug use among a group of intensive supervision probationers. The program had several key components including: 1) all new offenders were to be tested using a seven panel drug screen; 2) all offenders were to be tested at least twice per month; and 3) action was to be taken for all positive specimens.

A proactive process evaluation would commence at the start of the program to determine if the three components of the program were being implemented. The information would be used to make adjustments in the program (i.e., decisionmaking). The evaluator would determine if all new offenders received a baseline test consisting of a seven panel screen, if all offenders were tested at least twice per month, and if action(s) were taken for all positive drug tests.

If the evaluation was limited to an outcome evaluation, the first step would be to establish the integrity of the program. A retroactive process evaluation would be conducted to determine if the key components of the program had been implemented. If the key components of the program had been meet, then the outcome evaluation process should proceed and the success/failure of the program established.

If the outcome evaluation efforts were limited to outcome measures, the success of the program

could be decided using erroneous measures. If the components of the program had been implemented properly, the true success of the program could not be determined.

Object(s) of evaluation

Two factors should be kept in mind when answering this question: 1) Almost anything can be the object of an evaluation; and 2) the clear identification of the evaluation object is an important part of the evaluation design. The object of the evaluation will help establish the type of information to collect and how the data will be analyzed. The object(s) of an evaluation keep the evaluation focused. Clear object identification helps clarify and resolve value conflicts and potential threat among stakeholders.

After the evaluation object has been selected, a decision has to be made regarding the various aspects of the object that should be evaluated. A complete evaluation of a program is recommended. A complete evaluation of a program would include an assessment of (a) the merit of its goals, (b) the quality of its plans, (c) the extent to which those plans are being carried out, and (d) the worth of its outcomes.

Using information from the previous example, agency policies and procedures recommended all probationers entering the intensive supervision program be tested randomly at least twice per month for the first six months. The object of the evaluation would to determine if this policy had been achieved.

Criteria to judge object(s) of evaluation

The selection of the criteria with which to judge an object is one of the most difficult tasks in the evaluation. Goal achievement is often suggested as a criteria for an evaluation. This approach makes the selection of evaluation criteria easy; however, the validity depends on whether the goal was justified or worthy. Often trivial goals are established that are not worthy of achieving.

Evaluation criteria must be selected within the specific context of the object and the function of the evaluation. The evaluator is not solely responsible for selecting the evaluation criteria. However, the evaluator is responsible to see that a choice is made and that there is sound justification for the choice.

To follow-up on the previous example, the testing frequency for each probationer in the intensive probation program would be determined. The success of the urinalysis program would be determined by the percentage of probationers who were tested at the recommended frequency.

Audience(s) for the evaluation

An evaluation must be useful to a specific audience. The evaluation may have more than one audience. It is important to identify the specific audiences for an evaluation at the early stages of the evaluation because different audiences will have different evaluation needs. For example, probation/parole officers, adminstrators, and judges all have very different informational needs.

Evaluation steps and procedures

The steps and procedures involved in completing an evaluation will differ according to the perceptions guiding the evaluation. If the evaluation is conducted to determine if goals have been achieved, the following approach may be used:

1) State goals in behavioral terms
2) Develop measurement instruments
3) Collect data
4) Interpret findings
5) Make recommendations

If the approach of the evaluation is to provide information for decisionmaking, the evaluation process may include:

1) Identify decisionmakers information needs
2) Collect relevant information
3) Provide information to decisionmakers

All evaluations must involve interaction between the evaluator and their audiences at the beginning and conclusion of the evaluation. At the beginning of the evaluation, the evaluator will work with the audience to determine the evaluation needs. The audience will be involved at the conclusion of the evaluation to communicate the findings. Evaluations cannot be limited to data collection and analysis.

Selection of an evaluator

Should the evaluation be completed by an internal evaluator or should outside assistance be considered? A number of factors should be considered in making this decision. Are inside evaluators qualified, and do they have the necessary experience to handle an evaluation of this magnitude? What political pressures, internal and external, exist that would destroy an internal evaluation's credibility? What resources are available to conduct the evaluation? These and other questions should be considered in determining who will conduct the evaluation. Local universities are a good resource when searching for an evaluator.

The evaluation process

Brinkerhoff et al. (1983) in *Program Evaluation: A Practitioner's Guide for Trainers and Educators* outlined a seven step process for conducting an evaluation. The book was written with educators as the primary audience, however, the concept can be adapted to community corrections. Book chapters are based upon questions that should be answered during the program evaluation process. If administrators and evaluators consider each these questions, successful evaluations will be the result.

The seven steps in the evaluation process are: 1) focusing the evaluation; 2) designing the evaluation; 3) collecting information; 4) analyzing information; 5) reporting the results; 6) managing the evaluation; and 7) evaluating the evaluation. These topic areas will be used to suggest questions and/or areas of concern that the stakeholders and evaluator should discuss and come to agreement.

Focusing the Evaluation

Focus of the Evaluation

Even though this topic seems to be self-explanatory, agreement should be reached between the evaluator and interested stakeholders on exactly what will be evaluated. Will the evaluation be limited to a program, a group of offenders, specific staff, or the entire agency? Exactly what will the evaluation evaluate?

A complete description should be provided for the object to be evaluated. The description should include, but not be limited to: Who's involved? What goals and objectives are intended? What type of activities are included? How long has the object been around? What are the influences of the setting on the object?

By establishing "what will be evaluated," the evaluator and the administration have a complete understanding of the scope and/or limitations of the evaluation.

Purpose of the Evaluation

The general purpose of the evaluation should be clear. Is the purpose of the evaluation to determine if the goals and objectives have been met? Was the program designed in the most effective

manner? Was the program implemented properly? What are the outcomes and/or products of the program? How can the program be improved to more effectively meet the desired goals and objectives?

If the evaluator and the agency's administration establish a clear purpose for the evaluation, hidden agendas will be avoided. By establishing a clear purpose for the evaluation, other components of the evaluation process will become more clear.

Stakeholders in the Evaluation

Evaluation affects both the object of the evaluation and all who have a stake in the object. All stakeholders in the evaluation must be identified at this stage of the evaluation development process. It is usually not possible to accommodate all of the identified stakeholders, however, the information needs that can reasonably be accommodated should be considered.

Some of the audiences that should be considered are the sponsors of the evaluation, the sponsors of the program, key decision makers, and program participants. In the case of community corrections, it is critical that line staff be involved in the evaluation process.

Potential Influences on the Evaluation

There are a number of elements in the setting that could have an impact on the evaluation efforts. The type of management organization can assist or hinder an evaluation. Individuals within the leadership structure can influence the evaluation. The political structure within the organization, as well as the political structure outside the organization, can be helpful or harmful to the evaluation.

Other potential factors that can influence the evaluation are: the economical situation within the agency and the local community, resources available to the agency and the evaluator, history of the organization and/or the profession, and attitudes and opinions of the profession. If the profession is not completely open-minded to professional improvement, there are certain questions that should not be asked.

Evaluation Questions

Exactly what general questions will the evaluation address? As the evaluation design matures, the questions will be refined. The evaluation questions influence the kind of information that should be gathered, the means of gathering the information, and the analysis options.

At this stage the stakeholders must communicate clearly to the evaluator exactly what the evaluation should address. The evaluator may offer suggestions to assist in clarifying the administrator's evaluation objectives. The stakeholders' role is to clearly communicate the objective(s) of the evaluation efforts. The role of the evaluator is to assist the stakeholders to consider all possible options and to bring clarity to the evaluation objectives.

Potential for Successful Evaluation

At this point the evaluator and the stakeholders need to evaluate the potential for a successful evaluation. Key areas concerning the purpose of the evaluation, the research questions, and possible influences on the evaluation will have been discussed. If the evaluation does not have the potential for a successful completion, it may be a wise use of existing resources to delay or cancel the evaluation.

Designing the evaluation

If the agency initiates the evaluation, the agency stakeholders will play a major role in "focusing the evaluation." During this phase of the evalu-

ation, the stakeholders play the central role in deciding what will be evaluated, who will be affected, potential influences on the evaluation, the critical research questions, and the potential for a successful evaluation. The evaluator's role was to ask the right questions to make sure that all important elements were addressed.

If the evaluation was initiated by the evaluator or an outside agency, a similar procedure must occur to focus the evaluation. However, the evaluator may take more of a lead in discussing the purpose of the evaluation and the evaluation questions. Regardless of who initiated the evaluation, the administration and evaluator must discuss and come to an understanding on the questions relating to focusing the evaluation.

After the evaluation has been "focused," the design of the evaluation must be considered. The evaluator will take more of a lead in this discussion, however, all stakeholders must come to an understanding and agreement on the evaluation design.

Alternative Evaluation Designs

Every evaluation is made up of similar elements, however, these elements can be put together in many ways. There are three major decisions that need to be made at this stage.

Fixed versus Emergent Design. Can the evaluation questions and criteria be established at the beginning of the evaluation? If they can, they should be? This is a fixed design. An emergent design is one where the evaluation questions and criteria develop as the program and/or evaluation unfold. Both types have their advantages. Fixed designs can be adjusted as the evaluation progresses, however, most of the decisions are made in advance.

Process versus Outcome Designs. Should the evaluation have a process or outcome design?

Process evaluation designs evaluate the key components of the program. Outcome evaluation designs focus on "success" variables and are utilized after the fact. A process evaluation may be proactive. A proactive process evaluation would evaluate each step of the program and recommend strategies for immediate improvement. An outcome evaluation would start with a retroactive process evaluation to examine each step of the program, however, the overall focus of the evaluation would be "success" of the program.

Experimental and Quasi-Experimental versus Descriptive Designs. Will the evaluation include intervening in events or will it just "watch" events? If the desire of the evaluation is to be able to generalize findings to a larger population, experimental or quasi-experimental designs are in order. In experimental or quasi-experimental evaluation designs, subjects are randomly selected, treatments are randomly assigned, and measures of program impact are taken.

In some cases, intervention is not possible or practical. If events have already occurred, evaluators must use historical documents to conduct the evaluation. In other situations the evaluator may choose to watch, talk with people, keep a low profile during the data collection process, and describe what occurred.

Evaluation Design Components

All evaluation designs are composed of the same components. These components include focusing the evaluation, collecting data, analyzing the data, reporting information, and managing and evaluating the evaluation. What makes an evaluation more appropriate for a given situation is how well these basic features are integrated and operationalized.

Constructing an Evaluation Design

The keys to constructing an effective evaluation design are planning beforehand, involving key audiences, and determining the scope of the evaluation. The planning component was discussed in the previous section on "focusing the evaluation." Together the stakeholders and evaluation staff decide on what will be evaluated, the purpose of the evaluation, who will be involved/affected by the evaluation and the critical evaluation questions. Based upon these preliminary decisions, other key audiences should have the opportunity to provide input into the process. Final decisions should be made on the scope of the evaluation.

Based upon the planning conducted under the "focusing the evaluation" segment, possible research design selections will be narrowed. Other resource issues such as time, cost, and personnel for the evaluation should be considered when deciding on a research design.

Collecting Information

The data collection phase of the evaluation is more a function of the evaluator(s) and the evaluation staff, however, in many situations agency staff will be involved in the data collection process. This does not mean that the evaluator is solely responsible for the planning and execution of the data collection phase. Key evaluation stakeholders should assist in the planning of the data collection and must understand the complete process.

Type of Information to Collect

The type of information that should be collected are determined in part by the evaluation questions and the evaluation design. However, other factors also should be considered. What types of data are available?

Trade Offs in Performance Measurement				
Evaluation method	Steps	Strengths	Weaknesses	Best used when:
Process evaluations:				
Planned vs. Actual	Measure over or under targets	Least costly	<u>Measures process-es not results</u>. Targets may have no relationship to program effective-ness	You need to know if the processes are being deliv-ered according to design.
Outcome evaluations:				
1. Before/After comparison	Measure criteria before and after program	Low cost/low expertise needed	Low credibility; Difficult to link inputs to outcomes	Time and $ are limited; criteria stable over time
2. Time/trend projections of pre/post pro-gram	Measure criteria over several inter-vals and project future trends	Moderate costs and expertise	Extreme variations may falsely imply a trend	Historical data available/trend apparent;
3. Cohort com-parisons	Measures changes in similar groups where one got the program and one didn't	Low-moderate cost/time if data available otherwise moderate-high cost/time	Difficulty in find-ing matched groups raises validity issues	Comparison group is similar to pro-gram group. Randomized eval-uations impossi-ble.
4. Randomized	Identical groups randomly assigned to program or no program	Robust and system-atic method	High cost/time; very difficult	Where individuals will receive pro-gram services; where program effectiveness is critical

Adapted from Hatry, H. P. (1981). *Practical Program Evaluation for State and Local Government*. Urban Institute Press. p. 25-55.

What are the sources of information? What criteria should the information meet?

Data Collection

Again, the evaluation questions and design will dictate some of the procedures that will be used to collect the needed information. The key to selecting data collection procedures, is to select procedures that are simple and result in accurate data. Options for data collection involve qualita-tive and quantitative procedures. Qualitative procedures involve procedures such as case studies and transcripts. Quantitative procedures place information into categories.

Amount of Information to Collect

Only collect the amount of information that will be used. It is a waste of valuable resources to collect information you will not need or use.

If the evaluation involves a large population, random sampling is an effective method of reducing the amount of information that needs to be collected. Characteristics of a random sample can be generalized to the larger population. Proper techniques should be used to identify the sample size and randomly select the sample population. Every effort must be made to secure information from everyone in the random sample population.

Instrument Selection or Development

If instruments are available that meet the evaluation needs, they should be used. If instruments are not available, then the evaluator will have to develop instruments to meet the needs of the project. In both situations instrument validity and reliability must be addressed.

Information Collection

The key to getting the most information at the lowest cost is planning. Quality control must be maintained. If possible use one source for multiple questions.

Analyzing Information

Handling Returned Data

Who will receive the completed data collection instruments? How will the data be transformed into useful information? Who will enter the data into a computer readable format? All of these questions need to be addressed to insure data integrity.

Value of Data

The evaluator will examine the data before or immediately after it was placed into a computer readable format. Using experience and common sense, a decision will be made to determine if the data are worth analyzing. The data should

be cleaned and a random sample verified to establish its accuracy. Areas that could prevent further analysis are: incomplete responses, coding errors, low return rates, unusual responses, and/or administration and monitoring procedures were not implemented as planned.

Analyzing the Information

The data analysis procedures are dictated, in part, by the evaluation questions and the evaluation design. The data analysis procedures should be agreed upon during the planning process.

Data analysis should be limited to those procedures established during the planning process. If desired results are not achieved, some evaluators may want to continue the data analysis to find "a significant outcome." This procedure is frowned upon by reputable evaluators. If additional analysis is warranted after the initial data analysis has been completed, the evaluation stakeholders and evaluators should discuss and agree upon the additional procedures.

Interpreting the results

A few concepts should be kept in mind during the interpretation of the results. The first concept is the difference between statistical and practical significance. There may be statistical significance between two groups, however, the differences between the groups may not have any practical significance. The chances of statistical significance increase as the size of the population increases. An example is provided in the following. Ten thousand samples were tested for marijuana over a one year period. Group A average 2.2 specimens per month while Group B averaged 2.5 specimens per month. With the 10,000 specimens collected, the differences between the groups may be statistically significant, however, the differences between the groups on testing frequency has no practical significance.

The evaluator must report and attempt to explain any conflicting evidence. All findings must be reported. It is unethical to intentionally omit information.

The evaluator should only run the agreed upon statistical procedures. If the evaluator runs multiple statistical procedures, the chance of error increases, and the chance of erroneous by finding a statistical significance is increased.

Reporting Information

Evaluation Reports

The report audiences are the persons, groups, or agencies whose information needs and interests guided the evaluation or whose actions support the evaluation. The report format is determined by the audience. Should the report be written, oral, formal presentation, or news release? Many of these decisions should be made during the planning stage of the evaluation.

Report Content

The content of a report should be differentiated by the specific audience it was intended. Only give an audience what they need in a timely, direct and appropriate manner. Many times an evaluator will produce only one report and give it to everyone who has anything to do with the program.

Report Delivery

The ways to deliver a report may be different for each audience. Just as the content of the report was designed specifically for an audience, the delivery methods should also be designed specifically for the audience.

Appropriate Style and Structure for the Report

The style of the report will be geared to the specific audience. However, the following content should be considered; 1) abstract, 2) table of contents, 3) introduction, 4) body of report, 5) summary, and 6) closing.

Helping Audiences Interpret and Use Reports

Evaluation reports have the most impact when the reporting is constructed as a "dialogue" between evaluators and the audience. Develop a preliminary report and share it with some of the key audiences. Encourage these groups to provide feedback. Based upon the feedback, the evaluator will have some idea of how the information in the report will be interpreted and used. By clarifying problem sections of the report, an agency can avoid post-evaluation criticism of the evaluation techniques.

Managing evaluation

Managing the Evaluation

The responsibilities of the evaluator must be clearly defined. The responsibilities will be based upon the evaluation design, which in turn, reflects the evaluation questions. A job description or a list of responsibilities should be prepared. This list of responsibilities will allow the stakeholders to make various decisions about the evaluation and the role of the evaluator.

Evaluation Responsibilities

An evaluation agreement or contract should be developed to formalize evaluation responsibilities. This is critical if the evaluation is being conducted by an outside evaluator. The agreement/contract will specify what is to be done, how, when, and by whom. The process of contracting allows the evaluator and stakeholders to review the services that will be provided by the evaluator and the evaluation.

Evaluation Cost

An evaluation budget should be developed. The budget is the plan for acquiring and using financial resources to conduct the evaluation. Generally an evaluation budget includes the following: personnel (salaries and fringe benefits); consultants; travel and per diem; printing and shipping; conference and meetings; data processing; supplies and materials; and overhead (rent, utilities, telephone).

A rule of thumb for an evaluation budget -- it should be approximately 10 percent of the program or project budget. Like all rules of thumb, this is only a beginning point.

Organizing and Scheduling the Evaluation Tasks

A management plan begins when the evaluator and stakeholders are ready to sit down and ask, "What must be done, when, and by whom?" The plan that emerges provides a breakdown of tasks and a timeline for all those involved in the evaluation. The management plan charts the activities needed to implement the evaluation design and provides a system for keeping track of the progress.

The following information is needed to complete the management plan: specific activities that must be accomplished; when each activity is to be done; who will be responsible for the activities; how the activity will be accomplished; what resources are available to the do the evaluation; and the evaluation design or a general plan specifying what is to be done. The management plan should be updated as needed.

Problems to be Expected

The key issue in monitoring the evaluation is to make sure the design is still intact, relevant, and appropriate. Don't be afraid to change an evaluation design that is no longer meaningful. A regular review of the evaluation design with key stakeholders will keep the evaluation on track.

Evaluating Evaluation

Meta-evaluation?

A meta-evaluation, or evaluating the evaluation, will provide good information on the evaluation plans, designs, the evaluation implementation, and the evaluation's overall worth. Did the evaluation provide the needed information on the program? Was the information useful in recommending program changes? Was the evaluation design implemented properly? What problems were encountered with the evaluation design? Did the evaluator meet the conditions of the management plan and/or contract?

All of these questions address the merits of the evaluation, the evaluator(s), and the information received from the evaluation. Just as the results of a program were evaluated, the results of the evaluation should also be evaluated.

Conducting a Meta-Evaluation

The size of the program that is being evaluated will dictate who will conduct the meta-evaluation. The meta-evaluator must be competent enough to conduct the original evaluation and be able to tell if it was a good evaluation or a bad one.

If the evaluation was conducted by a team of evaluators, the team may conduct the meta-evaluation. Another solution is to hire an outside evaluator to conduct the meta-evaluation.

If the program being evaluated has a large budget, this is a possibility. However, if the program had a smaller budget, the evaluator and key stakeholders could meet and conduct the meta-evaluation. The final evaluation results could be sent to a panel of external reviews for a critique of the evaluation design and the evaluation results.

Summary

A number of key components for a successful evaluation have been discussed in this protocol. The evaluator and key stakeholders must decide upon answers to a number of key questions relating to these components to insure a successful evaluation effort. Brinkerhoff et. al (1983) in their *Program Evaluation* book outlined a number of these questions. They are:

Focusing the evaluation

What will be evaluated?

What is the purpose for evaluating?

Who will be affected by or involved in the evaluation?

What elements in the setting are likely to influence the evaluation?

What are the critical evaluation questions?

Does the evaluation have the potential for success?

Designing the evaluation

What are some alternative ways to design evaluation?

What does a design include?

How do you construct a design?

How do you recognize a good design?

Collecting information

What kinds of information should you collect?

What procedures should you use to collect the needed information?

How much information should you collect?

Will you select or develop instruments?

How do you plan the information collection effort to get the most information at the lowest cost?

Analyzing Information

How will you handle returned data?

Are data worth analyzing?

How will you analyze the information?

How will you interpret the results of the analysis?

Report Information

Who should get an evaluation report?

What content should be included in the report?

How will the reports be delivered?

What is the appropriate style and structure for the report?

How can you help audiences interpret and use reports?

When should reports be delivered?

Managing evaluation

Who should run the evaluation?

How should evaluation responsibilities be formalized?

How much should the evaluation cost?

How should evaluation tasks be organized and scheduled?

What kinds of problems can be expected?

Evaluating Evaluation

What are some good uses of meta-evaluation?

Who should do the meta evaluation?

What criteria or standards should you use to evaluate the evaluation?

If the key stakeholders and evaluator(s) provide answers to these questions during the evaluation planning process, the chances for a successful evaluation will be increased greatly. The likelihood of a misunderstanding between parties will be greatly reduced and a feeling of trust will develop. If there is trust among the parties involved, the profession will benefit.

REFERENCES

Alkin, M. C. (1969). Evaluation theory development. *Evaluation Comment 2*, 2-7.

Brinkerhoff, R. O., Brethower, D. M., Hluchyj, T., & Nowakowski, J. R. (1983). *Program evaluation: A practitioners guide for trainers and educators*. Boston: Kluwer-Nijhoff Publishing.

Cronbach, L. J. (1963, May). Course development through evaluation. *Teachers College Record, 64*, 672-683.

Hatry, H. P., Winnie, R. E., & Fisk, D. M. (1981). *Practical program evaluation for state and local governments*. Washington, D.C.: Urban Institute Press.

Joint Committee on Standards for Educational Evaluation. (1981). *Standards for evaluation of educational programs, projects and materials.* New York: McGraw-Hill.

Stufflebeam, D. L., Foley, W. J., Gephart, W. J., Guba, E. G., Hammond, R. L., Merriman, H. O., & Provos, M. M. (1971). *Educational evaluation and decision making*. Itasca, IL: Peacock.

Tyler, R. W. (1950). *Basic principles of curriculum and instruction*. Chicago, Illinois: University of Chicago Press.

RECOMMENDATIONS FOR AN EFFECTIVE MANAGEMENT INFORMATION SYSTEM

RECOMMENDATIONS FOR
AN EFFECTIVE MANAGEMENT INFORMATION SYSTEM

Squeezed by shrinking budgets and rising case-loads, community corrections agencies are searching for more efficient and effective ways to do business. Management information system capabilities are one of the essential components that cannot be ignored. To successfully implement a performance-based evaluation system, an agency must have in place an efficient method of storing and retrieving information in a useable format.

The successful implementation of a performance-based evaluation system is not dependant on an automated information system. However, without automation, sacrifices will have to be made in the way data are maintained, the timeliness of when evaluation results are reported, and the number of staff that need to be involved in the process. For the effective implementation of a performance-based evaluation system an automated management information system is recommended.

The remainder of this section focuses on the need for an efficient information system, as well as, an overview of the technical aspects of developing or improving an existing information system. Because of the dynamic nature of the computer industry, specific hardware and software recommendations will not be offered.

Rationale for an Automated Management Information System

In many situations probation and parole agencies are burdened with antiquated management information systems; in some instances a paper-based system is all that exists. A state-of-the-art information system offers agencies a number of advantages including:

- increasing the productivity of existing staff;
- handling the burden of increased caseloads;
- reducing paperwork drudgery;
- quick access to information; and
- maximizing time spent on case management activities.

With budget reductions and fewer dollars to spend on personnel, agencies are trying to find ways to get more work out of existing personnel. One way to do this is to reduce repetitive and redundant work. A study in Britain discovered, as an individual moved from arrest to incarceration, his name, date of birth, and address was entered on paper and computer as many as 17 times (Newcombe, 1995). Similar situations can be found in many information systems, including community corrections. Few community corrections agencies have the luxury of exchanging valuable information with other criminal justice and law enforcement agencies. By eliminating such duplication of effort, agencies can get more production out of existing staff.

An effective information system will also reduce and/or eliminate the paperwork process that can slow down a community corrections agency. This can reduce the drudgery of paperwork and improve overall employee moral. This reduction in paperwork will enable offices to focus more on effective case management.

The bottom line is that with an efficient information system, line officers will spend less time on paperwork and more time interacting with offenders on their caseloads. The increased level of contact will result in improved services for offenders and enhanced supervision practices.

A state-of-the-art information system also offers the opportunity for line officers to incorporate more efficiency into their supervision routine. For example, laptop computers could provide the officer in the field with a link to crucial information. Crucial supervision information can be temporarily stored on a laptop computer, or the laptop can be linked to the central information system via a phone modem, to provide line officers with instant access to pertinent information. Information gathered during field supervision can be entered into laptop computers and electronically transferred directly to the central information system. This eliminates a great deal of repetitive paperwork. To test the concept, a study was conducted with police officers in St. Petersburg, Florida and Los Angeles, California. Researchers concluded from the experiment that laptop computers have a role in field supervision and that the timely sharing of information is no longer a luxury in criminal justice (National Institute of Justice [NIJ], 1993).

Management Information System Issues

For those not familiar with the computer industry, computer jargon can be a foreign language. Terminology such as; CPU, pentium processor, MHz, megabyte, gigabyte, LAN, networking, baud rate, 486 processor, CD ROM, RAM, and ROM can intimidate the computer novice. Before you start the process of selecting hardware and software to implement or update an information system, you should develop an understanding of the basic terminology associated with the computer industry. There are a number of information sources that provide an explanation of computer terminology including a NIJ publication titled, *Use of Microcomputers in Criminal Justice Agencies* (McEwen, 1990).

Hardware: Administrators have two computer hardware options to consider in developing an

information system. The first option is to link a number of personal computers in a local area network (LAN). A stand-alone computer can be configured to handle the volume of data required by most information systems. Such a setup, however, does not permit simultaneous use of information. This limits the use of stand-alone personal computers in a modern information system.

State and local governments are buying PCs in record numbers and using them as a part of a LAN to share files and printers and to process information in a distributed environment. With powerful PCs and LANs, agencies are operating not only office automation programs, but imaging geographical information systems, and powerful relational database software for mission-critical applications (Newcombe, 1994). Personal computers, connected in a LAN, provide an inexpensive way to develop an effective information system.

The second option involves the use of a mainframe computer and accessing it with terminals at various strategic locations. Mainframe computers provide an effective information system. The cost of implementation and maintenance of the system, however, may be a disadvantage.

Software: Two options exist for the purchase of computer software. One, you can review off-the-shelf programs and select the one that best meets your agency's needs. The number of off-the-shelf software packages available for community corrections, however, is limited. Most departments have specialized management information system needs that cannot be addressed by generic software packages. It is however an expensive venture to have a computer software vendor personalize a commercial software package.

In addition to copyrighted commercial software packages, an agency should evaluate "public domain" software. "Public domain" software was developed with support from federal, state or local funding. The fact that a software package is "public domain" does not mean that it is free. Dissemination sources may charge for their support of the program, the cost of copying the program, and printing the documentation.

A second option is to contract with or hire a computer programmer to develop a program to meet the specific needs of an agency. The ideal situation would be to maintain a full-time programmer on staff to manage the information system needs. The programmer could tailor the information system to specific agency needs and be available to modify the system as information needs change.

Resistance to Change: While state-of-the-art information systems offer many advantages for community corrections agencies, there are still a number of obstacles that must be overcome. A major obstacle is resistance by administrators and staff to change. One way to overcome resistance to changes in the information system is to demonstrate the advantages to the new system to the agency. To reduce the level of resistance, representatives from all employee groups should be involved in the decisionmaking process.

Develop Policies and Procedures for Information System: A computerized information system presents several procedural issues. These issues include access to records, data coding schemes, permission to change records, ownership of records, and confidentiality of information. Policies and procedures must be established to provide guidance for administrators and staff in addressing these issues.

Policies and procedures should address various levels of access to information in the system. Everyone in the department should not have access to all offender information. A steering committee could assist in establishing various levels of security for the information system. Because personal computer LANs serve many functions in an agency (i.e., word processing, accounting, evaluation) and all employees usually have access to the LAN, security and level of access to the system are more of a problem than with mainframe-based systems.

The best situation for community corrections agencies is to participate in an information system shared by all facets of the criminal justice system. If this goal is achieved, agreements must be reached on consistent data coding schemes understood by all participants in the system.

In a multi-user information system, decisions will have to be reached on ownership of records and the right to change information in the record. Unauthorized changes can destroy valuable data. It is critical, therefore, that the system is protected from unauthorized record changes.

An underlying concept to all information system policies and procedures is the confidentiality of offenders' records. Policies and procedures should insure that authorized individuals have access to needed information, while unauthorized individuals cannot breach the confidentiality rights of offenders.

Summary

To establish an effective information system, a number of key questions must be answered during the planning and implementation process. These questions will provide agency administrators and steering committee members with essential information needed to make decisions relative to the implementation or improvement of an information system. The questions include:

1. What kinds of data are currently being collected?

2. What additional data fields need to be collected?

3. Are data available for additional data fields?

4. How will data be coded and entered in the information system?

5. Who is responsible for management and analysis of the information?

6. Will data retrieval and review be organized, fast, and accurate?

7. How often will data analysis/reporting procedures be conducted?

8. To what extent does the agency have the required software and hardware required for the information system?

9. Will written policies and procedures be developed for the information system?

Recommendations

1. To effectively implement a performance-based evaluation process, it is recommended that the agency implement and/or maintain an automated management information system.

    Few can argue with the advantages of a state-of-the-art management information system. Agency benefits in reduction of paperwork, minimizing duplication of data entry, and increased productivity of staff are far greater than the costs involved in implementing the system. Fast and accurate retrieval is essential for effective performance-based evaluation of community corrections programs.

2. Agencies should establish a committee to guide the implementation of an automated management information system.

    A management information system steering committee will accomplish two objectives. First, by involving representatives of key staffing groups in the decisionmaking process, employee buy-in can be enhanced and major resistance to change can be reduced or eliminated. Second, the steering committee can provide valuable information on agency needs and operating procedures.

3. Administrators and MIS committee members should carefully evaluate a number of management information system hardware and software options.

    Computer hardware and software prices vary greatly from vendor to vendor. It is important to "shop around." For example, in one agency a number of vendors were asked to provide bids on identical specifications for a 23 user DOS LAN. The difference between the lowest and highest bid was almost double. By examining several hardware and software options, the steering committee and administrators can select the best system for the agency at a fair price.

4. If someone on the staff is not experienced in information systems, a consultant should be hired to assist with the evaluation of agency needs and recommendations on hardware and software decisions.

    In many situations community corrections agencies have an individual(s) on staff with considerable computer expertise. If this is not the situation, it is recommended that a computer systems expert be consulted to examine agency needs and review vendor bids. This will ensure agency needs are addressed in all hardware and software purchases.

5. Management information system capabilities should be evaluated periodically.

Computer technology is changing rapidly. Periodically, the management information system should be evaluated to determine if additional hardware and/or software purchases could make the system more effective.

References

Camp, G. M., & Camp, C. G. (1994). *The corrections yearbook: Probation and parole.* South Salem, New York: Criminal Justice Institute.

Camp, G. M., & Camp, C. G. (1990). *The corrections yearbook: Probation and parole.* South Salem, New York: Criminal Justice Institute.

McEwen, J. T. (1990, May). *Use of microcomputers in criminal justice agencies.* Washington, D.C.: U.S. Department of Justice, National Institute of Justice.

National Institute of Justice. (1993, September). *Toward the paperless police department: The use of laptop computers.* Washington, D.C.: Author.

Newcombe, T. (1995, March). Information links the justice enterprise. *Government Technology, 8*(3), 1, 46-47.

Newcombe, T. (1994, May). Government on the LAN. *Government Technology, 7*(5), 1, 62, 64.

EXCERPTS FROM THE ANYTOWN, USA
COMMUNITY CORRECTIONS DEPARTMENT's
ANNUAL REPORT

Anytown, USA

Community Corrections Department

Excerpts from the

Annual Report

1994

1994 Facts on Adult Probation

Did you know:

.... **that** 98% of all offenders in the department were reassessed at least once each six month period?

.... **that** 74% of all offenders recommended for community supervision as part of the Presentence Investigation, successfully completed all probation/parole supervision requirements?

.... **that** 72% of all offenders in the department were employed full time during FY 1994?

.... **that** drug use violations for offenders in the ISP unit were reduced 11% from the fourth quarter of 1993 to the second quarter of 1994.

.... **that** 83% of offenders with treatment orders successfully completed their treatment program in FY 1994.

.... **that** a victim impact statement was completed for 97% of all offenses that involved a victim.

.... **that** 78% of all community service hours ordered during the first quarter of 1994 was performed by the end of the fourth quarter of 1994.

GOAL I: ASSIST DECISION MAKERS

PRESENTENCE INVESTIGATIONS

One of the goals established for the Anytown, USA Community Corrections Department was to provide information and recommendations to assist decision makers in determining appropriate disposition of cases. The presentence investigation (PSI) phase is one opportunity for probation/-parole officers to provide useful information to decision makers. All members of the Presentence Investigation Division strive to conduct complete and thorough investigations and provide the court with accurate and objective reports.

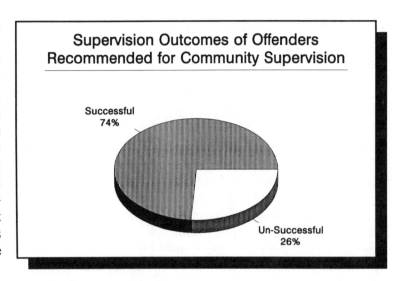

The Anytown, USA Community Corrections Department completed 2,340 presentence investigations during FY 1994. Seventy-two percent of the PSI recommendations were followed by the courts. Seventy-four percent of all offenders recommended for community supervision successfully completed their terms of probation or parole.

GOAL II: ENFORCE COURT/PAROLE BOARD-ORDERED SANCTIONS

REDUCTION IN DRUG USE

More offenders with higher levels of risks are being placed under some type of community supervision, often with more stringent conditions and court/parole board-ordered obligations. Probation and parole officers in the Anytown, USA Community Corrections Department are charged with the enforcement of these supervisory conditions. Enforcing court/parole board-ordered conditions is an important and difficult responsibility. It requires facilitation skills, ongoing monitoring, and timely responses to progress and noncompliance.

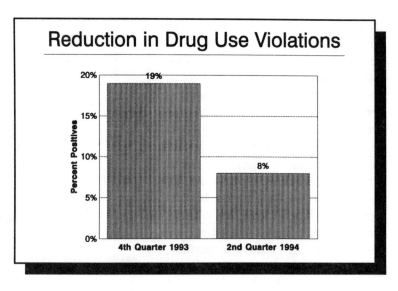

Approximately 72 percent of offenders under community supervision have a drug abuse problem. Many of these offenders are supervised by the Intensive Supervision Unit within Anytown's Community Corrections Department. These offenders are required to refrain from the use of illegal drugs. One method of monitoring compliance with this directive is the use of urinalysis. During the fourth quarter of 1993 there were 78 positive urinalyses results among the 409 offenders in the ISP unit. During the second quarter of 1994 there were 43 positive urinalyses among the 398 offenders remaining in this group. This represents an eleven percent (11%) reduction in drug use for this offender group over a six month period.

GOAL III: PROTECT THE COMMUNITY

ABSCONDING RATES

Protecting the community is an indisputable component of community correction's mission. While some may argue whether or not community corrections is in the business of behavioral change, few will argue whether or not protecting the community should be a driving force behind program development and operations within community corrections.

In order to protect the community from further criminal activity by offenders assigned to community supervision, the Anytown, USA Community Corrections Department

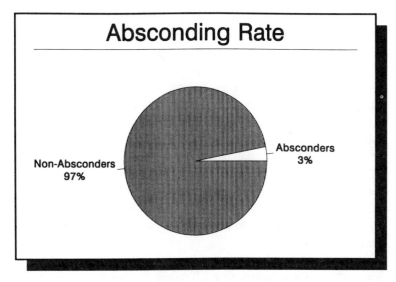

has initiated a number of assessment, intervention, surveillance, and enforcement activities. If an offender fails to comply with supervision conditions, appropriate steps are taken to insure compliance or community supervision is revoked. In order to monitor compliance, the department must maintain an appropriate level of contact with all offenders.

The rate of absconding serves as one indicator of supervision effectiveness. In 1994, 213 of the 7127 offenders (3%) supervised by the Anytown, USA Community Corrections Department were declared as absconders. Probation/parole and law enforcement personnel continue to try to locate these individuals.

GOAL IV: ASSIST OFFENDERS TO CHANGE

SUBSTANCE ABUSE PROGRAM

Substance abuse is a major problem among offenders in the Anytown, USA Community Corrections Department. Seventy-two percent of all offenders assigned to the department in FY 1994 were identified as having a substance abuse problem. Four treatment options exist in the local community: two inpatient and two outpatient programs. Of the 1678 offenders referred to the treatment options, 1437 (86%) were accepted. Four hundred and three offenders (80%) were accepted in the inpatient treatment programs and 1034 offenders (88%) were accepted for the outpatient treatment options.

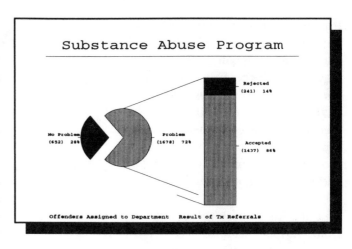

Nine hundred and ninety-five offenders from the Anytown, USA Community Corrections Department (69%) who were accepted for services, completed all requirements of their respective treatment program.

Urinalysis results and new arrests were examined for a 12 month period to determine the success of the treatment programs in changing offender behaviors. The rates of positive urinalysis for program participants ranged from 6-38 percent. The rate of new arrests ranged from 18-24 percent.

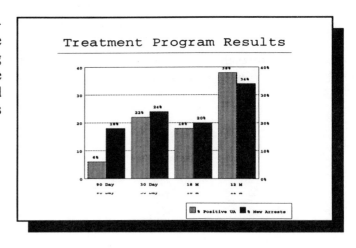

GOAL V: SUPPORT CRIME VICTIMS

VICTIMS SERVICES

The mission of the Anytown, USA Community Corrections Department includes the provision of support to crime victims. This support comes in the form of assessing the impact of the crime(s) on its victim(s), managing court-ordered restitution in order to improve the efficiency and effectiveness of restitution collection, and assisting in the protection of crime victims.

Seventy-four percent of all restitution scheduled to be paid during 1994 by offenders in the department was collected by the end of the year.

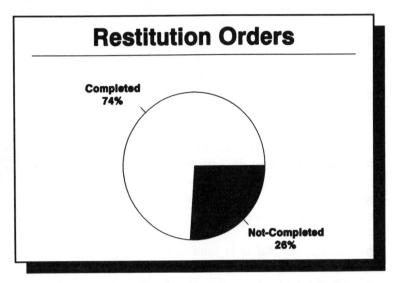

Sixty-eight percent of the crime victims surveyed were satisfied with the department's victims services program.

GOAL VI: COORDINATE AND PROMOTE THE USE OF COMMUNITY SERVICES

OFFENDERS ACCEPTED BY VARIOUS SERVICE AGENCIES

Offenders under the supervision of community corrections require a variety of services throughout their rehabilitative process. While many of these services are provided in-house, probation and parole agencies are still dependent on other community service providers to meet the offenders' needs. Cooperative planning between probation/parole and other community service agencies is essential.

The number of referrals and the percentage of offenders accepted for services were tracked as a measure of coordination and use of services.

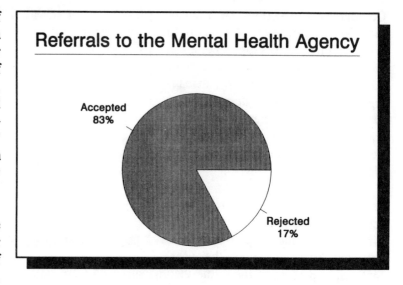

During the first quarter of 1994, 280 referrals were made to the local Mental Health Agency. Of the 280 referrals, 232 (83%) were accepted for services. For the 17% rejected for services, probation and parole officers attempt to meet the offender's needs through one-on-one counseling and problem solving.

SUMMARY OF 1994's GOALS, OBJECTIVES, AND RESULTS

Assist Decision Makers to Determine Appropriate Dispositions

Performance-Based Measure	Objective	Results	
PROCESS MEASURES			
Percent of PSIs completed on time.	95% of all requested PSIs will be completed on time.	96% of all PSIs were completed on time.	**Objective Achieved!!**
Degree of accuracy and completeness of PSIs.	90% of all PSIs will be complete and accurate when they are submitted to the court.	85% of all PSIs, evaluated by supervisors, were rated complete and accurate.	Objective was not achieved.
OUTCOME MEASURES			
Percent of offenders receiving recommended sentence.	75% of all offenders will receive the sentence recommended as a result of the PSI investigation.	79% of the PSI recommendations were accepted.	**Objective Achieved!!**
Percent of offenders recommended for and successfully completing probation/parole supervision.	70% of all offenders recommended for, and placed on, community supervision will successfully complete the conditions of probation or parole.	74% of all offenders recommended for community supervision during 1994, successfully completed their supervision requirements.	**Objective Achieved!!**

Enforce Court/Parole Board-Ordered Sanctions

Performance-Based Measure	Objective	Results	
PROCESS MEASURES			
Timely imposition of sanctions.	During the first quarter of 1994, officers will impose a sanction within five working days of a positive urinalysis result 90% of the time.	During the first quarter of 1994, officers imposed sanctions within five working days of a positive urinalysis result 75% of the time.	Objective was not achieved.
Number of revocation proceedings resulting from technical violations.	The number of revocation hearings, solely for technical violations, will be reduced by 5% for FY 1994.	For the first quarter, 26% of the revocations hearings were for technical violations. For the fourth quarter, 23% of the revocation hearings were for technical violations.	Objective was not achieved.
OUTCOME MEASURES			
Reduction in drug use violations.	The number of drug use violations as detected by urinalysis will decrease by 10% during the second quarter of 1994 for offenders assigned to the ISP unit in the fourth quarter of 1993.	Eleven percent (11%) reduction in drug use from the fourth quarter of 1993 to the second quarter 1994.	**Objective Achieved!!**
Percent of community service performed.	70% of all community service hours ordered during the first quarter of 1994 will be performed by the end of the fourth quarter of 1994.	78% of all community service hours ordered during the first quarter of 1994 was performed by the end of the fourth quarter of 1994.	**Objective Achieved!!**
Percent of favorable discharges.	80% of all offenders sentenced to community supervision will successfully complete the conditions of probation or parole.	67% of all offenders discharged from the department during the first quarter of 1994, successfully completed their supervision requirements.	Objective was not achieved.

Protect the Community

Performance-Based Measure	Objective	Results	
PROCESS MEASURES			
Percent of offenders reassessed according to agency policies.	90% of all offenders will be reassessed at least once during each six-month period.	98% of all offenders were reassessed at least once during each six-month period.	**Objective Achieved!!**
Percent of structured time.	60% of high risk offenders' time will be structured per week.	55% of John Jone's weekly time was structured.	Objective was not achieved.
OUTCOME MEASURES			
Average reduction in risk/need.	Six month offender reassessments will reveal an average reduction in risk/need of 10%.	During 1994 the average reduction in risk/need from initial to six month assessments was 12%.	**Objective Achieved!!**
Percentage of positive urinalyses.	The percentage of positive urinalyses for offenders in the Specialized Drug Offender Program will not exceed 20% during FY 1994.	The percentage of positive urinalyses for offenders in the Specialized Drug Offender Program was 28% during FY 1994.	Objective was not achieved.
Percent of treatment orders completed.	75% of offenders with treatment orders will successfully complete their program during FY 1994.	83% of the treatment orders were successfully completed in FY 1994.	**Objective Achieved!!**
Absconding rates.	The absconding rate for 1994 will not exceed 5%.	3% of the offenders absconded in 1994.	**Objective Achieved!!**
Rate of offender employment.	65% of all offenders will maintain full-time employment throughout 1994.	72% of offenders maintained full-time employment during 1994.	**Objective Achieved!!**
Percent of revocations due to technical violations.	Technical violations will account for 80% of revocations during 1994.	Technical violations accounted for 68% of revocations during 1994.	Objective was not achieved.

Assist Offenders to Change

Performance-Based Measure	Objective	Results	
PROCESS MEASURES			
Rates of attendance in outpatient treatment.	Overall attendance rates for the community outpatient treatment program will be no less than 75% during the first quarter of FY 1994.	The attendance rate for the first quarter of FY 1994 was 59%.	Objective was not achieved.
Degree of implementation.	80% of the case files for intervention planning and implementation will be rated as "fully implemented."	65% of the case files for intervention planning and implementation were rated as "fully implemented."	Objective was not achieved.
OUTCOME MEASURES			
Percent of offenders showing improvement in attitude.	70% of offenders participating in the domestic violence treatment group will show an improvement in attitudes.	49% of offenders participating in the domestic violence treatment group showed an improvement in attitudes.	Objective was not achieved.
Number of days drug free.	85% of the offenders successfully completing the inpatient treatment program during FY 1994 will remain drug free for a period of 90 days from the date of release.	75% of the offenders who successfully completed the inpatient treatment program during FY 1994 remained drug free for a period of 90 days from the date of release.	Objective was not achieved.
Level of improvement in controlling anger.	A three month reassessment of participants in Anger Control Groups during FY 1994 will reveal a minimum improvement of two rankings for 70% of the participants.	A three month reassessment of participants in Anger Control Groups during FY 1994 revealed a minimum improvement of two rankings for 75% of the participants.	**Objective Achieved!!**

Support Crime Victims

Performance-Based Measure	Objective	Results	
PROCESS MEASURES			
Percent of impact statements completed.	A victim impact statement will be completed for 95% of all offenses that involved a victim.	A victim impact statement was completed for 97% of all offenses that involved a victim.	**Objective Achieved!!**
Extent of planning and implementation to address victim's needs.	80% of the case files reviewed for victim service planning and implementation during FY 1994 will be rated as "fully implemented."	67% of the case files reviewed for victim service planning and implementation during FY 1994 were rated as "fully implemented."	Objective was not achieved.
OUTCOME MEASURES			
Proportion of restitution collected.	75% of all restitution scheduled to be paid during 1994 will be collected by the end of the year.	64% of all restitution scheduled to be paid during 1994 was collected by the end of the year.	Objective was not achieved.
Extent of victim satisfaction with agency victim services	80% of crime victims will rate agency victim services satisfactory at the time the offender completes supervision or has community service revoked.	68% of crime victims rated agency victim services satisfactory at the time the offender completed supervision or had community service revoked.	Objective was not achieved.

Coordinate and Promote Use of Community Services

Performance-Based Measure	Objective	Results	
PROCESS MEASURES			
Degree of interagency agreement implementation.	100% of interagency agreements between community corrections and community service agencies will result in ratings of "above average" or better.	67% of interagency agreements between community corrections and community service agencies resulted in ratings of "above average" or better.	Objective was not achieved.
Percent of offenders accepted by various agencies.	80% of offenders referred to service providers, will be accepted for services.	83% of offenders referred to service providers, were accepted for services.	**Objective Achieved!!**
OUTCOME MEASURES			
Progress of offenders in community service agencies.	80% of all offenders will make satisfactory progress in service programs as measured by monthly progress reports.	71% of all offenders demonstrated satisfactory progress in services provided by community service agencies.	Objective was not achieved.
Percent of offenders satisfactorily completing service.	60% of all offenders referred to domestic violence treatment will satisfactorily complete the program.	52% of all offenders referred to domestic violence treatment satisfactorily completed the program.	Objective was not achieved.

1995 PRIORITIES

Many significant achievements were made by Anytown, USA Community Corrections Department. The Anytown, USA Community Corrections Department is committed to the ongoing improvement of its operations. For 1995, the following priorities have been established:

- improve the accuracy and completeness of PSIs;

- impose sanctions in a more timely fashion;

- increase the percentage of offenders who maintain full-time employment;

- take steps to improve attendance in outpatient treatment;

- improve the percentage of restitution collected from offenders; and

- increase the number of offenders who satisfactorily complete the domestic violence treatment program.

Decision makers rely on information from probation/parole officers to determine appropriate dispositions of offender cases. In 1994, 85% of the PSIs evaluated by supervisors, were rated complete and accurate. This fell short of the 90% goal. PSI officers and supervisors will review the findings from the PSI evaluations, and determine what actions should be taken to improve the accuracy and completeness of PSIs in 1995.

For reinforcement/punishment to be the most effective, it must be immediate and directly linked to the activity. In 1994, sanctions were imposed within five working days of a positive urinalysis 75% of the time. In 1995, officers and supervisors will work toward improving the timely imposition of sanctions to 90%.

In 1994, the Department established a goal of maintaining full-time employment for 65% of its offenders. This goal was achieved and surpassed when 72% of the offenders in the Department maintained full-time employment. Because of the relationship between employment and success on probation/parole, employment will remain a priority for the department. In 1995, the goal is for 77% of offenders in the Department to maintain full-time employment.

In 1994, attendance rates for community outpatient treatment programs were 59%. Through cooperation with the treatment providers, appropriate supervisory visits with offenders, and the timely use of technical violation procedures, the staff of the Anytown, USA Community Corrections Department will work to improve the attendance in community outpatient treatment programs to 75%.

In 1994, 64% of scheduled restitution payments were collected from offenders. In 1995, emphasis will be placed on ways to improve the collection of restitution payments. The goal for 1995 will be to collect all restitution payments prior to the successful release of 75% of the offenders.

With local and national attention focused on domestic violence, the Anytown, USA Community Correction Department must do its part to help eliminate the problem. In 1994, only 52% of referrals resulted in successful completion of the program. In 1995, 60% of all offenders referred to a domestic violence treatment program will successfully complete the program.